Paul Tillich's Philosophical Theology

Other Palgrave Pivot titles

Madhvi Gupta and Pushkar: **Democracy, Civil Society, and Health in India**

Alistair Cole and Ian Stafford: **Devolution and Governance: Wales between Capacity and Constraint**

Kevin Dixon and Tom Gibbons: **The Impact of the 2012 Olympic and Paralympic Games: Diminishing Contrasts, Increasing Varieties**

Felicity Kelliher and Leana Reinl: **Green Innovation and Future Technology: Engaging Regional SMEs in the Green Economy**

Brian M. Mazanec and Bradley A. Thayer: **Deterring Cyber Warfare: Bolstering Strategic Stability in Cyberspace**

Amy Barnes, Garrett Wallace Brown and Sophie Harman: **Global Politics of Health Reform in Africa: Performance, Participation, and Policy**

Densil A. Williams: **Competing against Multinationals in Emerging Markets: Case Studies of SMEs in the Manufacturing Sector**

Nicos Trimikliniotis, Dimitris Parsanoglou and Vassilis S. Tsianos: **Mobile Commons, Migrant Digitalities and the Right to the City**

Claire Westall and Michael Gardiner: **The Public on the Public: The British Public as Trust, Reflexivity and Political Foreclosure**

Federico Caprotti: **Eco-Cities and the Transition to Low Carbon Economies**

Emil Souleimanov and Huseyn Aliyev: **The Individual Disengagement of Avengers, Nationalists, and Jihadists: Why Ex-Militants Choose to Abandon Violence in the North Caucasus**

Scott Austin: **Tao and Trinity: Notes on Self-Reference and the Unity of Opposites in Philosophy**

Shira Chess and Eric Newsom: **Folklore, Horror Stories, and the Slender Man: The Development of an Internet Mythology**

John Hudson, Nam Kyoung Jo and Antonia Keung: **Culture and the Politics of Welfare: Exploring Societal Values and Social Choices**

Paula Loscocco: **Phillis Wheatly's Miltonic Poetics**

Mark Axelrod: **Notions of the Feminine: Literary Essays from Dostoyevsky to Lacan**

John Coyne and Peter Bell: **The Role of Strategic Intelligence in Law Enforcement: Policing Transnational Organized Crime in Canada, the United Kingdom and Australia**

Niall Gildea, Helena Goodwyn, Megan Kitching and Helen Tyson (editors): **English Studies: The State of the Discipline, Past, Present and Future**

Yoel Guzansky: **The Arab Gulf States and Reform in the Middle East: Between Iran and the "Arab Spring"**

Menno Spiering: **A Cultural History of British Euroscepticism**

Matthew Hollow: **Rogue Banking: A History of Financial Fraud in Interwar Britain**

Alexandra Lewis: **Security, Clans and Tribes: Unstable Clans in Somaliland, Yemen and the Gulf of Aden**

Sandy Schumann: **How the Internet Shapes Collective Actions**

DOI: 10.1057/9781137454478.0001

palgrave▶pivot

Paul Tillich's Philosophical Theology: A Fifty-Year Reappraisal

George Pattison

Chair of Divinity, University of Glasgow, UK

palgrave
macmillan

DOI: 10.1057/9781137454478.0001

First published 2015 by
PALGRAVE MACMILLAN

Palgrave Macmillan in the UK is an imprint of Macmillan Publishers Limited, registered in England, company number 785998, of Houndmills, Basingstoke, Hampshire RG21 6XS.

Palgrave Macmillan in the US is a division of St Martin's Press LLC, 175 Fifth Avenue, New York, NY 10010.

Palgrave Macmillan is the global academic imprint of the above companies and has companies and representatives throughout the world.

Palgrave® and Macmillan® are registered trademarks in the United States, the United Kingdom, Europe and other countries.

ISBN: 978–1–13745–448–5 EPUB
ISBN: 978–1–13745–447–8 PDF
ISBN: 978–1–13745–446–1 Hardback

A catalogue record for this book is available from the British Library.

A catalog record for this book is available from the Library of Congress.

www.palgrave.com/pivot

DOI: 10.1057/9781137454478

Contents

Preface

The invitation to write this book came as an opportunity to pay a debt of gratitude – to Paul Tillich. It was largely (though not solely) through undergraduate work on Tillich that I got a foothold in the world of German Idealism that has been a large part of my intellectual life ever since. Perhaps no less important is that, in Tillich's case, this meant German Idealism in its critical confrontation with the kind of radical Marxism associated with the Frankfurt School – Horkheimer, Adorno, Marcuse, and others – that had been such an important element in the political milieu of the 1960s. Tillich therefore helped me to see, as perhaps few others could have done, how and why the fundamental questions that arise from attempting to think about God in our cultural situation are interlinked with both philosophy and radical politics. As chapters or sections of my *Art, Modernity and Faith* (1992), *Anxious Angels* (1999), *God and Being* (2011), and *Eternal God/Saving Time* (2015) show, he has also remained a continuing point of reference in much of my subsequent work. As I shall argue in the body of this book, there are aspects – central aspects – of Tillich's thought that are problematic in the light of more recent intellectual developments (not least vis-à-vis the debate about ontotheology and the growing demand for a post-metaphysical approach to God), but *at the very least* Tillich retains the power to remind us of just what is at stake in these debates. Tillichian theology was never just 'academic' but always *pensée engagée* and that should remain a fundamental *desideratum* of any serious thinking about God.

DOI: 10.1057/9781137454478.0002

List of Abbreviations

For full publication details see Bibliography.

AA *On Art and Architecture*
CB *The Courage to Be*
EN *The Eternal Now*
GW (volume number) *Gesammelte Werke*
IH *The Interpretation of History*
LPJ *Love, Power, and Justice*
NB *The New Being*
PE *The Protestant Era*
PNTT *Perspectives on Nineteenth and Twentieth Century Protestant Theology*
RS *The Religious Situation*
SD The Socialist Decision
SF *The Shaking of the Foundations*
ST (volume number) *Systematic Theology*

palgrave▶**pivot**

www.palgrave.com/pivot

Introduction

Abstract: *Introduction identifies the relationship between theology and philosophy as the focus of the work. Where Tillich speaks of standing on the boundary between these disciplines it is suggested that, as we encounter it in his thought, this relationship is more of dynamic mutual transformation.*

Pattison, George. *Paul Tillich's Philosophical Theology: A Fifty-Year Reappraisal.* Basingstoke: Palgrave Macmillan, 2015. DOI: 10.1057/9781137454478.0004.

▶

Fifty years after his death, Paul Tillich (1883–1965) remains a significant and controversial point of reference for Christian thought. Although a cursory glance at the catalogue of a university library is likely to show the number of books about Tillich going into steep decline in the 1970s, there are signs of a resurgence of interest. There are a number of reasons for this and, strikingly, recent work on Tillich spans a wide range of subjects. At one end of the spectrum are works relating him to the highly technical and abstruse debates about ontotheology that have been central to recent work in the continental philosophy of religion (I shall say more of these later and will explain the bewildering term 'ontotheology'). At the other are studies showing how his work helps Christian thought in engaging with a range of arts, including the popular art of filmed entertainment. There has also been interest in his political engagement and in the application of his thought to questions of Christian doctrine as well as to cultural phenomena ranging from film and technology through to business studies.[1]

This short study will focus especially on the tension between philosophy and theology in Tillich's thought. In an autobiographical essay entitled *On the Boundary*, published shortly after his emigration to the United States of America, introducing his thought to a new, American readership, Tillich described his life and work as situated at a series of boundaries, 12 in all, including the boundary between theology and philosophy. Of this particular boundary he wrote: 'The border-situation from which I am endeavoring to explain my existence, is in no way more openly revealed than here' (IH, 30) and, as he goes on to tell his readers, his career had been marked by a more or less continuous oscillation between the faculties of theology and philosophy. Qualified in both subjects, he was a theologian in Halle and Berlin, a professor of 'the science of religion' in Dresden, returning to theology in Leipzig, and, in his last position in Germany, moving again to philosophy in Frankfurt, where he was closely associated with the beginnings of the Frankfurt School of Critical Theory. After moving to America, his main teaching activity was in Union Theological Seminary in New York, although he retained important connections to philosophy and other areas.

This might, of course, be taken as a sign of indecision and Tillich's 'oscillation' could perhaps be glossed as 'vacillation' – but, as he himself emphasized, none of these changes involved an essential change in the main focus of his intellectual interest, nor in the way in which he approached his central subject matter: the question of religion. In

DOI: 10.1057/9781137454478.0004

fact, it might be taken as one of the possible complaints against Tillich that his thought did not really develop over time but simply involved the application of a few key formulae to ever-new subject matter. Of course, this might equally well be put in positive terms: that Tillich was a thinker who stayed true to his own principles through a series of massive personal, historical, and intellectual convulsions and that such constancy is in itself no bad thing. Indeed, it might just be what many people look for in someone who professes to teach religious truth. And this, we need to hold constantly in mind, was a man who, as an army chaplain, lived through one of the most terrible battles in human history (Verdun) in which hundreds of thousands of soldiers were killed, and someone whose opposition to Nazism led him into exile and a new life in a new language and a radically new cultural situation. An outlook that can sustain a person through such changes might be thought to have something going for it.

As far as this study is concerned, however, the question is not primarily a biographical question about whether Tillich the man was true to himself. Instead, it is about whether his intellectual position was intrinsically capable of maintaining its own defining insights, withstanding relevant criticism, and appropriately incorporating new elements without surrendering its own principles. In short, was Tillich's intellectual consistency justified in the light of the internal coherence of his thought and of its ability to respond to external challenges?

And here we should immediately note another aspect of the question, implicit in Tillich's own image of being 'on the boundary'. This suggests – to my mind unfortunately – that when we are dealing with the relationship between philosophy and theology we are dealing with two fixed entities in such a way that the only question is where exactly the boundary between them lies and whether, or how far, it is legitimate to cross from one to the other (and if, having crossed over, it is then possible to go back). In these terms, Tillich here seems to perpetuate a widespread use of such geo-political metaphors in 'mapping' the relationships between different academic discourses, whether, as in Kant's essay entitled *The Conflict of the Faculties*, it is a matter of the higher or lower faculties or whether it is about where the line is to be drawn between human, social, and natural sciences and then, within each discipline, what divides one 'field' or 'area' of study from another. However, it is important to remember that all of this is, essentially, metaphorical. Even if academics sit and work in physically separated locations, the reality of

DOI: 10.1057/9781137454478.0004

their work is frequently – perhaps even mostly – more fluid than such divisions might suggest.

Returning to Tillich's own 'boundary-situation' I am suggesting that despite the apparently static nature of the 'boundary' metaphor, a theology that is in significant dialogue with philosophy is itself developed through this dialogue and vice versa. When in my title I speak of Tillich's philosophical theology, then, this is not to be taken in the sense that, in the end, Tillich the theologian triumphed over Tillich the philosopher (or that he was really a theologian all along and only a philosopher on the surface). It is rather to point to a certain transformation of philosophy itself in which the philosopher becomes one who speaks about God and does so with the commitment we associate with the idea of theology but on the basis of philosophy and not by adherence to any particular confessional position. In Tillich's case the picture is further complicated by the fact that his philosophy is itself developed through a transformative engagement with theology – and not just with academic theology but with the kind of practical theology that arises out of ministerial office involving pastoral care and preaching. The point is therefore not an attempted reinstatement of theology as 'Queen of the Sciences' (though some theologians have recently called for this), but the exploration and furtherance of a continuing struggle to establish the concept of God and the reality of religious life as dynamic elements in an existential attitude that has fully internalized the experience of modernity and the philosophical heart of the modern experience. At its very simplest, I take this to be a question of the relationship between being and love, a relationship that might be envisaged in terms of a movement from a philosophical discourse focused on being to a theological discourse focused on love, but which might alternatively be conceived as a movement within philosophy itself. But what such a movement means or could mean, what problems it raises, and whether Tillich's way of effecting this move is finally persuasive are issues that can only be resolved – or, at any rate, moved forward – in the substance of the book itself.

Note

1 For example, J. Brant, *Paul Tillich and the Possibility of Revelation through Film* (Oxford: Oxford University Press, 2012).

1

'God Is Being-Itself'

Abstract: *Starting with Tillich's definition of God as Being-Itself, the chapter traces this idea back to Tillich's early study of Schelling and the latter's move from a philosophy of identity to a philosophy of freedom. However, despite existential elements, Schelling's thought remains fundamentally limited by the philosophy of identity. It is argued that the same can also be seen in Tillich's own system. Although this is published 40 years after the early work on Schelling, it reflects the same basic structures of thought. This makes it problematic in the wake of postmodern philosophy, which (following Heidegger) emphasizes difference against identity.*

Pattison, George. *Paul Tillich's Philosophical Theology: A Fifty-Year Reappraisal.* Basingstoke: Palgrave Macmillan, 2015. DOI: 10.1057/9781137454478.0005.

We begin with a word that is absolutely central to the thought of Paul Tillich, as well as to understanding what is at issue 'on the boundary' between philosophy and theology – the word: God. At first glance, what Tillich says about this seems very clear. God, Tillich says (and he says it in many places), is 'Being-Itself'.[1] Furthermore, he insisted that this is a 'non-symbolic' statement and, in fact, the *only* non-symbolic statement we can make about God. Everything else we might say about God – such as that God is 'Father' or 'Lord' or 'Creator' or 'Trinity' – is symbolic, only not this. We shall come back to Tillich's theory of symbolism at a later stage,[2] but I shall begin by attempting to clarify just what is at stake in this insistence on Being-Itself as a definitive claim about the meaning of the word 'God'. For if Tillich is clear that God is Being-Itself, the claim itself is not as clear as the simplicity of its language suggests and many of Tillich's readers have found it profoundly puzzling. What does it – what *can* it – mean?

First, strange as this formulation might seem to many believers and, for that matter, non-believers, Tillich is at this point reflecting a long-standing tradition of Christian thinking that goes back through medieval theology to Augustine and beyond. Thomas Aquinas, whose teaching is regarded as normative in the Catholic Church, asserts that 'He Who Is' is the best of the names we can give to God and his reason for saying this is that he too, like Tillich, regards 'Being' as definitive of the divine nature. In fact, both Thomas and Augustine use the same formulation 'Being-Itself' (*ipsum esse*) as Tillich.

If this seems remote from the language of living religion – and it is, undeniably, influenced by Greek philosophy as well as by biblical thought – it is nevertheless not hard to see that it does say some of the things that believers want to say about God. For if God is supposed to be the source of all that is, then God must surely *be* in some eminent sense? And – a point made by Thomas – the insistence on *being* also makes it clear that God does not come into being or pass out of being; God simply *is* as he is, eternally, without change. Only a God who truly is Being-Itself is a God we can rely on in all the changes and chances of life in this world. And, if a biblical proof-text is wanted, Augustine, Thomas and others pointed to the story of how God called to Moses out of the Burning Bush and, when Moses asked God to tell him his name, God (in the version made familiar by the King James Version) replied: 'I AM THAT I AM'.[3] As one hymn puts it, God is, simply, 'the great I AM'.

In later chapters, we shall have occasion to revisit the religious and philosophical purchase of these claims. First, however, I want to look more closely at the philosophical background of the claim that God is Being-Itself and do so in the light of Tillich's own intellectual context and development. Doing so will also throw light on the consistency of Tillich's thought over many years and through many upheavals. It will also help to explain Tillich's commitment to the idea that theology has to be systematic, in the sense that every theological statement had to make sense in relation to every other and that this requires theology to develop a specific structure and shape. This commitment is unusual in modern Protestant theology – not least when this theology also bears the epithet 'existential'.

Tillich and German Idealism

If Tillich's use of the expression 'Being-Itself' is connected to ancient traditions of Christian thought, his particular usage was more immediately shaped by his relation to German Idealism. This was a movement that developed in the 1790s, both influenced by and reacting against Kant's critical philosophy. It flourished through to the 1830s before being overtaken by new movements in the 1840s (e.g., the 'Left Hegelianism' of Feuerbach and Marx and the proto-existentialism of Kierkegaard), although these often reflected some of the Idealists' claims or methods. One of the most enduring aspects of his kind of Idealism was its sense that philosophy didn't just drop ready-made from heaven and that doing philosophy involved reckoning with the history of philosophy. Indeed, it was central to the claims of Hegel and Schelling, two of its leading figures, that their thought summed up and recapitulated the preceding history of philosophy before moving decisively beyond it. Importantly, their idea of this history embraced not just philosophy in the narrow sense but also extended to great religious movements, such as the rise of Christianity in opposition to ancient Judaism and paganism or – another key example in their view – the Protestant Reformation. This entailed several significant differences in their approach compared to that of medieval thought.

First, they saw medieval philosophy as having failed to take fully seriously the subjective side of human knowledge. Thus, in the case of a universal term such as 'goodness' the medievals (on their view[4]) tended to think that this existed somehow independently of anybody actually choosing to do good (or not). Likewise in the case of 'being', 'Being' was

DOI: 10.1057/9781137454478.0005

'there', so to speak, whether any individual actually existed (or not). But, the Idealists argued, we have learned (in different ways) from Descartes, Hume, and Kant (amongst others) that the structure of our minds always affects what we know. If there is a mind-independent reality out there, we can only know it in the prism of the human mind. And goodness, as Kant in particular argued, cannot exist independently of moral action itself – goodness is less something 'there' and more something we *do*. True knowledge is both objective and subjective and philosophy, therefore, must at least give an adequate account of both aspects – which medieval thought failed to do.

But the issue was not purely philosophical, it was also religious, and here the event of the Protestant Reformation loomed large in the minds of the Idealists. Even though Schelling would convert to Catholicism, he, like other important figures in the movement (including Fichte and Hegel), had been trained in Protestant theology and some of their theological assumptions continued to shape German Idealism as a whole. As they saw it, the early Protestant movement arose out of the disintegration of what has been called 'the medieval synthesis'. In the late medieval period, a complex of changes meant that individuals became increasingly isolated and the modern spirit of subjectivity began to push to the fore. But, as Martin Luther experienced with particular intensity, this brought with it a massive sense of anxiety and guilt. When the authoritative teaching of the Church and the moral mechanism of the penitential system began to lose their grip, individuals came to experience themselves as isolated, worthless and, in theological language, desperately sinful. For Luther, the agony of this situation could no longer be eased by turning to the Church and making ritual acts of confession and reconciliation. The kind of assurance he needed could only be given by God himself, more specifically the God revealed in Jesus Christ, crucified as a sacrifice for human sins. No longer mediated by what has been called 'the great chain of being' or by the idea of gradually climbing the ladder of perfection up towards God, Luther's faith involved something like a one-to-one confrontation between guilt-ridden sinners and a God who could move between a terrible, punishing righteousness and the self-sacrificing love revealed in Christ.

What all this meant to the German Idealists was that it was not enough to write subjectivity into their account of knowledge. Just as crucial was the need to recognize that the subject in question, the human being, was not just a knowing subject but also a feeling, suffering, yearning subject, a subject of desire whose life was exposed to the terrifying prospect of guilt and death. Philosophy had to take account of the whole human being and not just the mind. And if the term 'system' sounds abstract to our postmodern ears, part of the point of insisting that philosophy had to be systematic was to emphasize that, in Hegel's words, 'the truth is the whole' – that is, the *whole* human being in the *whole* of its bodily, historical, intellectual, and religious development.

Being born when he was (1886) and educated in philosophy and theology in the German academic system it was inevitable that Tillich would be exposed to the thought of the German Idealists. Of course, as I have indicated, there were already strong contrary voices making themselves heard from the 1840s onwards, including Marx, Kierkegaard, and Nietzsche, each of whom would have a significant impact on Tillich. Yet his own initial choice was to focus on Schelling – not least because he, like others, saw Schelling's own later development as pointing beyond itself towards what Schelling himself already called 'existential' elements. In fact, Tillich wrote two major early works on Schelling, a doctorate in philosophy *The Construction of the History of Religion in Schelling's Positive Philosophy* (1910), and a theological dissertation *Mysticism and Guilt-Consciousness in Schelling's Development* (1911).[5] We shall examine this latter work now, since, I shall suggest, it effectively offers a blueprint for Tillich's own system, even if this would also go on to incorporate elements or be applied in ways that reflected Tillich's distinctively twentieth-century experience and that would have seemed quite alien to Schelling himself.[6] It will, in particular, help us to clarify what Tillich might have meant by defining God as 'Being-Itself'.[7]

A further reason for beginning with this dissertation is that it will help us to see that Tillich's existentialism was not just the result of encountering the philosophy of Martin Heidegger in the 1920s (as is often said), but that it had an independent source and, as a result, a rather different shape from Heidegger's own 'philosophy of existence'.[8]

Mysticism and Guilt-Consciousness in Schelling's Development

A key term in the dissertation is 'identity', since Schelling's early philosophy had been known as a 'philosophy of identity' and his later thought was generally seen as modifying this in significant respects. We shall therefore begin by briefly examining this term, which will, incidentally

DOI: 10.1057/9781137454478.0005

but importantly, establish a point of reference for assessing the relevance of Tillich's own thought to some contemporary issues in the philosophy of religion.

So what is meant, in this context, by identity?

Think back to God's disclosure of the divine name to Moses: I AM THAT I AM. Such a statement could well serve as an epitome for the philosophical principle of identity, namely, that something is simply what it is. In a formula favoured by the Idealists themselves, A=A. As Tillich put it in commenting on Schelling's notion of identity, the absolute isn't a *syn*-thesis, it's just a thesis (GW1, 36). But if A=A seems self-evidently true, it also seems to be something of a *cul de sac*. Where might philosophy go from here? How does this tautology help us to solve or even understand actual questions about what it is to know something? If we are challenged as to how we know that this object in front of us is a tree, surely it's the most unphilosophical attitude possible just to say 'because it's a tree: a tree is what it is', which is what applying the principle of identity would seem to amount to. Nevertheless, the Idealists' ambition was, starting from this self-evident formula, to deduce the entirety of the human system of knowledge.

This might seem a strange ambition. However, what was at stake was, in some respects, quite simple, namely, the very possibility of truth. If I want to say anything true about the world, then, it seems two conditions must hold. The first is that the propositions in which I make such statements must be free from ambiguity and internally coherent. In the statement 'The dog is a star' both terms are, potentially, ambiguous. I might be referring to the celestial body known as 'the dog', in which case (as Spinoza pointed out), the term 'dog' is being used metaphorically. On the other hand, I might mean that the dog (individual member of the species *canis canis*) has performed an action I regard as admirable. But, in either case, in order to decide whether what is being said is true my listener would need to translate the metaphorical elements of the statement into direct, unambiguous terms – what some philosophers refer to as the requirement of univocity; that is, saying just one thing and saying it without ambiguity. If, on the other hand, we once allow an element of equivocation we would never really know whether what was being said was true or not. The second condition is that what is said really is true. To vary the example, if I say that the dog is black, then this is only true if the dog *really is* black. Even if the statement 'the dog is black' fulfils the condition of logical possibility, it is not true if the dog in question is a Golden, rather than a Black Labrador. This is what medieval philosophers meant when they maintained that truth is the adequation (or correspondence) between what is in the mind (*mens*) and the thing at issue (*res*). What is said or thought must, in an important sense, be *the same* as what is being spoken or thought about. The double condition for anything at all being true is therefore that the totality of all possibly true propositions must submit to the logical requirements of consistency and univocity and that there is a fundamental conformity between the mind that thinks and the world that is thought about. The basic claim in any system of identity, then, is that philosophy can show that this is indeed the case, that is, that we can construct a system of knowledge that is logically seamless and that represents the world as it really is.

But there is a further element in the picture that was of crucial importance to the German Idealists. For although they deviated from Kant at a number of points they broadly accepted his emphasis on the primacy of practical reason, that is, the will to bring about the highest good. In terms of the formula A=A this meant that the challenge was not just to give an account of knowledge (A) as merely offering a truthful reflection of how things really are (A) but of how, when A=the will, this relates to A=the object of willing. In fact it was precisely this active aspect of thought that provided the Idealists with the key they were looking for and that helped them to establish the principle of identity. They suggest that when we realize that the absolute is not primarily identifiable with a contemplative mind or a static state of being but with an active will, then – precisely then – we can see that its unity is a free act of self-affirmation. It can be at one with itself because it freely wills to be at one with itself. I may be able to acquire a true knowledge of the tree outside my window, but I didn't choose that it should be there or that there should be trees in the world at all – but I can (it seems) choose to think about what I want to think about. If knowledge of external objects always implies a certain gap between knower and known or subject and object, wilful self-affirmation simply is the affirmation of the self as it is: I AM THAT I AM.

However, in the world in which we human beings live and move and have our being, freedom seems to be limited in all manner of ways. What I want to do is blocked or inhibited by a manifold of phenomena that stand over against me and that Fichte collectively referred to as the 'Not-I', including even my own mental habits and dispositions. Consequently, the absolute will that wills itself and its world in unbroken

DOI: 10.1057/9781137454478.0005

unity and self-identity can only appear under material and historical conditions as an infinite or progressive approximation. On the whole, however, the German Idealists glossed this situation in an essentially optimistic manner, portraying history as a history of freedom progressively gaining mastery over the Not-I (i.e., its material and social environment), and thereby revealing the world to be 'a moral world-order' physically structured in such a way as to facilitate the infinite expansion of freedom.

The early Schelling offered two important modifications to this model, both of which can be connected to his influence on the Romantic Movement in Britain and America as well as in Germany. These are his emphases on nature and on art. With regard to nature, Schelling suggested that rather than thinking of nature merely as a kind of material Not-I standing over against human subjectivity (like the tree outside my window), we would do better to think of it as itself an expression of Spirit. In these terms, then the encounter of I and Not-I in the human experience of nature is actually the reciprocal attraction of Spirit in nature and Spirit in human being. In being one with nature, we become one with the divine Spirit that is the living power of nature itself. Another way of putting this difference is that the Spirit that is creatively active in nature is unconscious, and it becomes conscious in human experience of nature.

But at what point or how do these two types of experience, conscious and unconscious, become one? Schelling's answer is that the eminent form in which we experience this coincidence is art, since artistic creativity is a form of mental life that is both unconscious (it is not a matter of conscious planning or control) and conscious (it is a real, fully mental event). 'Unity with God is reached in aesthetic experience of nature' (GW1, 45). This also has the corollary, which becomes important for Tillich, that whereas Fichte's insistence on the progressive realization of freedom essentially rewrites the Enlightenment's belief in human beings' capacity for self-perfection, Schelling's nature mysticism allows for an analogy of what religion calls 'grace', that is, an experience that is given to us from beyond the orbit of our conscious ideas and choices.

However, as Tillich puts it, what this amounts to is 'the effective substitution of religion by the mysticism of art'. The genius now becomes the source and focus of divine revelation, even though – with regard to the unconscious aspect of creativity – he himself cannot explain all that he sees or how he sees it: he is a human being living under the same particular conditions as anybody else and yet, at the same time, he is 'inspired by an other breath' (GW1, 57). As expounded by Tillich, then, we can start to see how, despite setting out to offer a system of identity, Schelling does so in such a way as to make this system dependent on something essentially irrational, such as the unconscious impulses that produce the visionary experience of the poet.

Schelling's own way of dealing with this tension was to develop an account of what he called 'the potencies'. Rather than God (or the absolute) being directly manifested in nature and freedom, Schelling postulated a sequence of what he called 'potencies' (or powers) that mediate this manifestation in a progressive way. The potencies active in nature are the mechanical, dynamic, and organic potencies whilst those active in the ideal world are knowledge, action, and art. At the summit of this sequence, the human being is open to and can freely combine all the potencies, being both a natural and an ideal being (i.e., a being defined both by its biology and its mental life). In the phenomenon of the human being who adequately realizes the interconnected structure of divine potencies, then, the universe reveals its highest form of life and, as Tillich comments, the human being is thus seen, effectively, as God (GW1, 64). More concretely, this means that rather than focusing on the solitary figure of the artistic genius, Schelling now looks to the whole living community of culture in which the life of a national community finds self-expression (GW1, 65).

This is all very up-beat. But, Tillich now asks (as he believes, Schelling also started to ask) whether, if the world of ideas really did constitute a self-identical whole, would it really need to express itself in nature and history in this way? Why wouldn't it just enjoy the bliss of its eternal self-identity? Conversely, doesn't any kind of consciousness in fact imply difference as well as identity? Knowing the dog to be black, I acknowledge that I am not the dog and I can, in fact, only know the dog to be black in a world in which dogs are black, and white, and grey, and brown, and many other colours besides. Even in the case of an object of will, that I will or intend some object implies that this object is not already fully and perfectly realized here and now or not in the way that I am willing it. As Tillich explains, Schelling himself starts to speak of a 'fall' of the world of ideas, breaking away from their unity with or in the absolute into a world of things, contingencies, space, and time. The I of the self-conscious creative human being is therefore a curiously mixed phenomenon: because it is just this 'I' it is marked by singularity and contingency – but

DOI: 10.1057/9781137454478.0005

it can also become the point at which the fallen world is returned to and reinstated in the prototypical world as its temporal and historical life is transformed and reconciled through science, art, and moral action in which the totality of experience is gathered together and apprehended as an intellectual whole.

Nevertheless, the more seriously we look at history, the less plausible a 'mystical' system of identity becomes. If the philosopher believes himself capable of seeing the unity of history, this unity is only ever fully realized in the world of ideas, not in space and time (GW1, 69). And, as Tillich points out, if we talk about the sequence of potencies as 'progressive' this is only in a hierarchical rather than a temporal sense and so, even if the doctrine of the potencies enriches the abstract idea of God, it still falls short of mediating the divine unity and the manifold of real historical events. Moreover, Schelling's approach seems to be modelling moral and historical achievement on the pattern already seen in the artist and thus morality and religion too become a matter of genius. Those Schelling calls 'men of God' are described as acting 'on the grand scale and entirely, without care for what is individual' (GW1, 71) and might seem to anticipate the Nietzschean 'supermen'. And, since their genius is misconstrued as a necessary manifestation of reason, it seems that there is no scope for error or guilt. To speak of sin or lack is merely to misperceive what is 'really' a single, unified manifestation of divine reason. But, again, this conclusion seems not to do justice to what we experience as the real and intractable difficulties of life.

As Tillich reads Schelling, however, these are not just objections made from without, but they are also tensions of which Schelling himself became aware and which he attempted to address. Thus, in what Tillich calls Schelling's 'second period', the philosopher attempts to expand or overcome the system of identity so as to give an adequate account of freedom, including the freedom to will what is not determined by necessity or reason. Now Schelling insists increasingly on the claim that 'Willing is primordial being (*Ursein*)' (GW1, 78) and that the existence of the absolute 'is in all eternity: act' (GW1, 78).[9] The unity of the system is no longer a matter of simple identity but of identity freely willed and chosen in opposition to everything that might threaten to tear it apart: 'In the absolute synthesis, essence completes itself in self-positing over against absolute contradiction, freedom against necessity, the rational against the irrational, light against darkness. But this synthesis is God' (GW1, 79).

DOI: 10.1057/9781137454478.0005

This also means that, in an important sense, the absolute must be a personal, self-conscious being or, more precisely, a being in whom conscious and unconscious, freedom and necessity, rationality and irrationality are conjoined. In this way, Schelling can speak of nature as, somehow, 'in' God – but, the claim is, this is not pantheism (the teaching that God and nature are identical), since God's freedom is more than mere nature. God is God because he eternally makes himself God and chooses himself as the God whose life is manifested in nature and history. Consequently, and crucially, it is in the phenomenon of the human microcosm that the personality and freedom of the divine life become manifest as such.

Has God therefore been reduced to a cipher for humanity? No, Schelling suggests, because, at the same time, there is that in God that is prior to any manifestation. The statement that 'God is Lord' can be taken as Schelling's protest against simple mysticism. In God there is a '*Prius* of Godhead, being that exists before all thought (*unvordenkliches Sein*), the sheer "that"' (GW1, 84). This precedes all rational conceptions of God and all manifestations of God in nature or history. As Lord of Being, God is '*Über*'-being – 'beyond being', we might say. But this means that instead of attempting to deduce the structure of divine being from an abstract principle such as A=A, philosophy cannot do more than attempt to follow and describe the ways in which the divine life has actually manifested itself. This shift from *a priori* deduction to what we might call phenomenology is also called by Schelling a shift from negative philosophy, that is, philosophy that abstracts from life, to positive philosophy, that is, philosophy that, tracking the actual occurrence of life is also able to give an account of freedom.

Nevertheless, if Schelling is now seeing God himself in terms of a dynamic process in which all the contraries of necessity/freedom, and so on, are fully and freely synthesized, there remains a tension that was already implicit in the system of identity. As Schelling sees it, this 'process' is, somehow, always already – 'eternally' – completed in the life of God 'above the contradiction of time and timeless fixity' (GW1, 87). But in history, in actual life, we experience real and outstanding differences that are still to be overcome. Crucially, this is focused in what human beings experience as sin, that is, the occurrence of what-ought-not-to-be. In God, the division of good and evil is always already resolved in favour of the good, but precisely because the life of the creature is distinct from the inner life of God, the possibility of good and evil is a

DOI: 10.1057/9781137454478.0005

constant accompaniment of human life. In wanting to exist as free and independent individual beings, we necessarily separate ourselves from the unity that is fulfilled in God. An individual tree, of course, is also 'different' from God, but the human individual is not just 'different' but freely and deliberately wills or chooses to be 'himself' or 'herself' – and this is the basis of sin, which is 'contradiction that has become Spirit', that is, a self-conscious manifestation of life that chooses to be itself in its separation from God (GW1, 88).

Sin is not rationally necessary. It can be freely overcome and subjected to the good. If it claims to be a permanent and integral element in the universe, these claims are essentially mendacious. Yet sin does point to the fact that life has been, as it were, handed over to time, to 'the absolute other of eternity' (GW1, 91). But it is time that also reveals the limitations of sin and exposes its mendacity when the creature that has defined itself through sin is brought, by time, to the realization that, *qua* individual, it must necessarily die.[10] All things must pass, of course, but what in nature is simply fate is experienced in human life as a matter of guilt. Because it is separated from God the 'I' that I am or have made myself to be is, as such, sinful – a thought that Tillich sees as underlying the idea of a 'transcendental fall' prior to any particular sinful acts. Sin is much more than a matter of sins (avarice, sloth, pride, etc.) since it is rooted in the very identification of my 'I' with my isolated particular self. This means that, as Kierkegaard stated, 'The normal relation of the human being to God is repentance' (GW1, 20–1). But Tillich nevertheless resists what he calls the heterodox view that the substance of human life is as such originally fallen, since, even in the state of separation, there remains a consciousness of God. Paradoxically, therefore, the reality of sin becomes evidence for God (GW1, 96)!

But how might the 'I' that has in this way become separated from God and from the good be restored to its original unity with God and learn to see its entire life as manifesting the divine will? If it is really to heal the condition of a being that has made itself into a particular, individual being, such an act of restoration must, Tillich suggests (still following Schelling), also become an event in an individual personal life. Furthermore, since what is made manifest in this event is the divine will to overcome evil with good and since, also, the divine will is nothing other than the divine being itself, the overcoming of sin must take the form of God himself becoming an individual human personality who gives those who have separated themselves from God the possibility of re-entering into communion with Him. And, because it is death – above all unnatural death – that reveals the true reality of sin, such a divine Incarnation must also go all the way to death: the Cross. And although Tillich does not at this point invoke the specifically Kierkegaard notion of paradox, he does speak of the Cross as 'the highest contradiction' (GW1, 97).

In eternity, we recall, primordial time and end-time are united and mysticism has 'always already' triumphed over guilt and separation. But, in history, this unity has to be worked out in time as the transition from what-ought-not-to-be to what-ought-to-be. Over and above the evolution of social order, science, and philosophy, Schelling takes this as indicating that the meaning of history is fulfilled in the history of religion, since religion offers the supreme representation of what-ought-to-be. As told by Schelling, the history of religion shows a progression from the mythical religions of wrath to the Greeks' philosophical mysticism of pantheistic unity that is, in turn, opposed by Judaism's anti-mystical stance. The dialectic between pagan mysticism on the one hand and Jewish guilt-consciousness and Messianism on the other is then synthesized in Christianity as the triumph of grace over contradiction: 'The principle of mysticism triumphs, but not in the form of mysticism, not as immediate identity, but as the personal community in which contradiction is overcome, i.e., "the religion of Spirit and freedom"' (GW1, 108). This can also be expressed as the emergence of love as 'the meaning of the world-process' (GW1, 98).

Tillich's Schellingian system

In the forty years between his dissertation on Schelling and the publication of Volume I of his *Systematic Theology*, Tillich's life and thought passed through many upheavals – war service, civil anarchy, and exile being merely the outer markers of what many would regard as a tumultuous life. Yet although many new elements would be taken up into Tillich's thought in this time, we can see that the broad shape of his system was already established in the dissertation and if we had to sum up the thrust of his mature thought we could scarcely do better than to repeat the conclusion of the dissertation, that it was the proclamation and defence of 'a religion of Spirit and freedom'. Perhaps unsurprisingly, then, some of Tillich's own reservations vis-à-vis Schelling can be

DOI: 10.1057/9781137454478.0005

rephrased as potential criticisms of his own system. Before returning to these criticisms, however, let us first briefly note some of the major points of continuity.

The first, and most obvious, is contained in both the title and the conclusion of the dissertation. Tillich's system itself is a system incorporating and synthesizing a basic tension between mysticism and guilt-consciousness, that is, a tension between the inner identity of all that exists with Being-Itself and the simultaneous separation of all that exists, in existence, from Being-Itself.

That God is Being-Itself is the one non-symbolic statement we can make about God (Tillich says). But, of course, Being-Itself is not an object amongst objects. Although we see innumerable things that exist or that *are*, we never get to see Being-Itself. As Hegel puts it, if we go into a shop and demand fruit, we will only ever get a choice of apples, oranges, or pears but never 'fruit' as such. By the same token, Tillich points out that whenever we do speak about God and say anything more than the tautology that God is Being-Itself, then we cannot help making God into some kind of object, no matter how intellectually refined or subtle. This is because we cannot think of anything without making it into an object. 'The theologian cannot escape making God an object in the logical sense of the word,' writes Tillich, 'just as the lover cannot escape making the beloved an object of knowledge and action' (ST1, 191). But this brings with it the risk of turning God into an object amongst objects, and if that happens then God 'ceases to be the ground of being and becomes one being among others' (ST1, 191); '*a* being, [who] is subject to the categories of finitude, especially to space and substance' (ST1, 261). It is in this sense that whilst the gods of paganism (Zeus, Aphrodite, Thor, etc.) are indeed beings that can, as Tillich says, be 'experienced, named, and defined' (ST1, 235), the God who is truly God is, in an important sense, a 'God above God' and even 'above' the God of Christian theism itself (CB, 176–83).

But if God is, in this sense, outside or beyond the totality of beings that, together, make up the world 'and all that therein is', because God is Being-Itself (or, as Tillich also likes to put it, the ground or power of being), no individual exists or can exist except by participating in some way in being, that is, in God. Being-Itself, Tillich insists, is not just a static being that is entirely simple and self-contained (like the absolute in the system of identity) but, like the God of Schelling's later 'positive philosophy', exists as a dynamic and living synthesis in which all that exists is freely and eternally reconciled. Otherwise all we could say about it would indeed be an empty tautology – 'being is'.

If Being-Itself is to become knowable then it can do so only in a differentiated and structured way and the most obvious and unavoidable example of such structuring is the subject–object structure of knowledge itself. I cannot know anything or even experience anything at all unless I am, in some degree, a subject capable of knowing and unless what I know presents itself, in some way, as an object capable of being known. Although innumerable gradations on both sides of the subject–object relationship are possible, some minimum must in each case be present. Of course, as we have just seen, a God who is knowable is therefore in some sense or in some degree made into an object of human thought and, as a result, is no longer God in an absolute sense. All 'knowledge' of God is consequently 'symbolic', although theology has long been aware of this and has developed strategies for building awareness of its own imprecision into what it says about God. If we try to get outside the subject–object schema, however, then, as Tillich puts it 'reason looks into its own abyss ... in which distinction and derivation disappear' (ST1, 193).

Over and above the subject–object division, however, Tillich sketches a sequence of polarities that is implicit in every manifestation of being that we can experience or know. These somewhat resemble Schelling's divine potencies in that they seem to mediate between the ineffable depth of Being-Itself and the emergence of a world in which being can be manifest and, like the potencies, these polarities do not constitute a historically progressive sequence but are timeless and *a priori* – no matter how varied their expression may be. The three key polarities are individualization and participation, dynamics and form, and freedom and destiny.

Although we might first think of individualization as a specifically human phenomenon, Tillich makes the point that nothing can actually exist unless it is in some way individualized – this tree, this rock, this sunset. Yet, at the same time, nothing can exist unless it also participates in a larger reality. Tillich did not live to witness the expansion of ecological thinking, but he would certainly have understood the point that, in these cases, trees, rocks, and sunsets are what they are only by virtue of their being interconnected in manifold ways with their overall environment and history. But all of this is especially true of human beings. On the one hand, our capacity for becoming self-conscious means that we can reach a degree of individualization unknown elsewhere in the

DOI: 10.1057/9781137454478.0005

universe, yet Tillich argues (again like Schelling) that this same consciousness gives us the ability to participate in all that exists. This participation is especially manifest in reason and language, through which,
as he puts it, 'the universal structures, forms, and laws [of the world]
are open to [the human being]' (ST1, 195). In this sense he re-affirms
the Renaissance idea, repeated by Schelling, that the human being is a
microcosm in whom the truth of the entire cosmos is recapitulated and
made manifest. The highest form of individualization and participation
is when the human individual becomes a fully developed person and,
as such, is able to enter into a full personal communion with others. No
one could really be a person in complete isolation, since, for example,
sympathy, thinking, and speaking (which might be taken as conditions
of being a fully developed person) can only be developed in and through
relation to others.

A similar pattern of interdependence can be seen in the case of
dynamics and form. As Tillich says, '"Being something" means having
a form' (STI, 197). Something that was completely formless wouldn't
be anything. Yet nothing drops from heaven ready-made, so to speak,
and perhaps we know even better than Tillich's generation that whether
we are talking about chemical elements, animal species, or the history
of ideas everything is what and as it is by virtue of a dynamic process
of development. But, as Tillich points out, this was already recognized
by philosophers who lived long before the discovery of evolution. In a
sentence that brings together a number of key terms, Tillich writes of
this dynamic aspect that it is generated by 'the *mē on*, the potentiality
of being, which is non-being in contrast to things that have a form, and
the power of being in contrast to pure non-being' (ST1, 198). In other
words, anything that is a definite something is what it is by virtue of having become what it previously was not, and what it now is will, at some
future point, cease to be. In the language of mythology and of various
previous philosophies this is variously described in terms of the chaos
preceding creation in Genesis 1, the *Urgrund* spoken of by Jacob Boehme
and incorporated by Schelling into his system, Schopenhauer's will, and
Nietzsche's will-to-power as well as Bergson's *élan vital*. The distinction
of dynamics and form is itself, as Tillich also notes, formulated as such
by Aristotle. Importantly, and in this instance against the medieval theological adaptation of Aristotelianism, this means that it is just as limiting
to think of God as pure act or perfect form as it is to think of Him as an
object. God is and is beyond both dynamics and form.

DOI: 10.1057/9781137454478.0005

Freedom and destiny prove to be likewise interdependent. As Tillich makes it clear, however, this is a relationship in which the structure of ontological polarities reaches a limit and a turning point. The advent of freedom in human existence opens the way to a new relation to being and this is also why Tillich chooses to speak of freedom and destiny rather than freedom and necessity. Where necessity might be seen as inherently opposed to freedom, destiny suggests the possibility of a certain reciprocity, as when we imagine some great historical figure, a Napoleon perhaps, freely choosing to embrace his destiny. Only a being that is essentially free can have a destiny: 'Come the hour, come the man.'

Alongside these polarities and conditioning, how they actually appear in the world is the further distinction of essence and existence. At its simplest, this is the distinction between what something is and that it is. I can, for example, say just *what* a Dodo is even though, as a matter of fact, no Dodos now exist. On the other hand, I might become aware of a newly discovered object that no one (yet) knows whether to call a bird or a beast. In this case we know *that* it exists but not *what* it is. However, in the case of something that is both known and that exists, we find ourselves having to acknowledge that the fact of existence introduces a certain distinction into the essence. In Aristotelian terminology, the essence or nature of a tree is never fully or completely realized in the existence of any individual tree. And, as we have seen in Schelling, it is one thing to put forward a system of identity that deals solely with the ideal or essential relationships amongst its elements but it is quite another to try to incorporate what is individual and particular and, in the case of human existence, is also endowed with self-will. In terms of the schema of polarities we have just surveyed, a thing exists only when its potential for being what it is becomes fully actualized – the acorn becomes an oak. But since potentiality is also equated by Tillich with relative non-being (*mē on*) this means, as he puts it, that 'existence means standing out of non-being' (ST2, 23), also playing on the etymology of to ex-ist, namely, 'to stand out of'. And, in the case of human beings (as we have now several times seen), this also involves the wilful and therefore also in some degree free act of self-choice or self-affirmation.

But if this all sounds very technical and abstract, it has some immediate and massive theological implications. For what it seems to imply is that we cannot exist as human beings without, in some way, separating ourselves out from our own essential being. In order really to exist we

DOI: 10.1057/9781137454478.0005

must break with the divine world of self-identical ideas or essences, that is, 'what' God would have us be, and this, in effect, means that what Genesis and Christian doctrine describe as the fall of human beings into a state of sin coincides with the mere fact of existing. Creation and fall cannot be separated in the way in which traditional doctrine separated them when it spoke of a good and perfect creation that was only subsequently rejected by human beings through an act of voluntary disobedience. In Tillich's vision it seems that, as in Schelling's system, *any* voluntary act is going to separate us from the divine unity and, since we cannot be human except through affirming our capacity for voluntary action, to exist as human means to be separated from God. Drawing on Kierkegaard's account of the fall, Tillich explains that human beings cannot remain in a state of dreaming innocence but, via an anxious awareness of their own greater possibilities, are led to choose individuation at the price of unity with their divine ground. As Tillich sums up 'The state of existence is the state of estrangement' (ST2, 51).

In this situation of estrangement, however, something else happens. Although the polarities of being (individualization and participation, etc.) are necessary for there to be a structured world at all, the self that has become separated or estranged from the ground of its being experiences the relationship between them as distorted and conflictual. Far from helping us to construct a liveable world, they become structures of destruction (ST2, 69ff.). The individual no longer experiences community as supportive or enabling but as threatening or remote, 'them'. Form is seen as 'mere' form, as in artistic formalism that conveys no sense of life or vitality or behaviour that is required solely 'for form's sake', whilst the necessary element of 'dynamism' degenerates into chaos when it is separated from form. Finally, freedom separated from destiny becomes sheer arbitrary wilfulness, the defiance of the rebel who simply refuses to do whatever anyone else wants him to do, whilst destiny becomes necessity, requiring the simple and complete submission of anything that might try to oppose it.

In commenting on Schelling, we saw that Tillich resisted the apparent implication of Schelling's system that made the fall inevitable. But what about his own system? Hasn't he done just that? Hasn't he presented us with a picture of human existence in which, it seems, we are ceaselessly tossed between one-side individualism and oppressive collectivism, between formalism and anarchy, or between rebellion and submission? But if this is a plausible picture of what human life in the world is actually

DOI: 10.1057/9781137454478.0005

like, doesn't it jar with the fundamental Christian conviction that creation is good as such and human life in particular 'very good'?

Crucial to Tillich's whole strategy at this point is the insistence (which we can again already see in the Schelling dissertation) that if human self-affirmation does indeed involve separation from the divine ground, this separation or estrangement is never absolute. Even when they are transformed into structures of destruction, the ontological polarities are inescapable and the world as a whole and human life within it, as its microcosm and highest instance, continue to bear the traces of their divine origin. And this will be true as long as they exist, since they cannot exist unless, at the same time, they participate in Being-Itself. Without such participation, they quite simply could not be. As Tillich puts it in *The Courage to Be*, published the year after the first volume of the *Systematic Theology*, even 'if we do not know [the power of being], we nevertheless accept it and participate in it' (CB, 176). No matter how deeply separated we may have become from our essential being and no matter how fragmented and conflicted our lives may have become, we retain an implicit sense for what would make us whole. The isolated individual wants love, the empty formalist craves depth and content, the chaotic child unconsciously yearns for boundaries, and so on. Nevertheless, in the situation of estrangement, we cannot give ourselves what we need. In art or utopian imagery we can envisage how a fulfilled life might look but mostly, it seems, we cannot attain it. Consequently, the restoration of unity can only take place when God himself freely chooses to draw near and reveal this 'new being' in a fully personal human life, creating possibilities of communion in the midst of alienation and estrangement – and, once more, this is precisely the same solution that Tillich had, forty years before, found in his study of Schelling. If existence means estrangement, the state of estrangement itself points the way towards the fulfilment it needs and is therefore never without hope. In the life of God, fulfilment is always eternally present and we, even in our state of estrangement, are never excluded from the possibility of participating in that eternal fulfilment (ST3, 449–52).

There is much more to be said about Tillich's account of the forms taken by estrangement in the historical experience of his own time and of how this estrangement might, quite concretely, be overcome, and exploring these themes will take up much of the following chapters. In them, we shall see how the philosophical basis of his thought is transformed into theology, but I shall end this chapter by briefly looking at one possible philosophical critique of Tillich's position.

A Heideggerian criticism

If, as I have suggested, the outline of Tillich's thought can already be found in his early studies of Schelling, then Heidegger is correspondingly less important as a source for his distinctive version of existentialism. This is not to deny a number of commonalities, which are scarcely surprising given the fact that these exact contemporaries were exposed to a range of similar intellectual influences, including Greek philosophy, Christian theology, German Idealism and nineteenth-century historicism. But the fact that they inhabited the same world of thought also makes it possible to look to Heidegger to indicate a line of criticism of Tillich's ontology that, at the same time, will help us see more precisely just what is at stake, philosophically and theologically, in Tillich's specific formulations.

As its title suggests, Heidegger's *Being and Time* sees the question of Being as essentially related to the human experience of time. Time, as he puts it, is taken to be 'the possible horizon for any understanding whatsoever of Being'.[11] In other words, there is nothing we can experience or say about Being that is not in some way coloured by the fact that we are utterly temporal beings. But this also means that since being temporal is, as Heidegger puts it, to be 'thrown' towards annihilation in death, the meaning of Being appears only in relation to our own prospective death.

Now Tillich says something similar. The question of Being, he says, only ever arises as the reflex of metaphysical shock that he also calls 'the shock of possible non-being' (ST1, 181). This shock is the realization that, *qua* individual existent, I am thrown, ineluctably, towards death and, in death, will absolutely cease to be. Again, we shall come back to further aspects of this situation in later chapters, but we need immediately to note a significant difference in Tillich's approach in comparison with that of Heidegger. For Tillich, as we have seen, the shock of non-being and the experience of estrangement do not imply that we are absolutely separated from Being-Itself and therefore from the divine life, in which all difference and estrangement is eternally overcome. For Heidegger, however, the radical experience of temporality reveals that all talk of eternity is essentially empty. In a famous footnote, he criticizes Kierkegaard for making the typical theological move of attempting to explain the meaning of time by reference to eternity. No. As far as *Being and Time* is concerned we are nothing but time, and time and time alone sets the horizons for what we can experience, think, and hope for.

In a much later lecture, 'The Principle of Identity', Heidegger too starts off from the German Idealists' attempt to deduce the whole structure of reality from the tautological principle A=A.[12] However, as he proceeds, it becomes clear that, in his view (and here too the entire temporal structure of human existence plays an important implicit role), strict identity is always going to be elusive. All human experience, all human discourse, is marked by a certain play of difference. Going back to what was said at the start of this chapter about the basic aims of a philosophy of identity, Heidegger saw the scholastic belief in a complete adequation of thought and being as impossible to realize. There will always be a certain unbridgeable gap between them. The attempt to impose a fully unified identity, however, involves what, in a related lecture, he calls 'ontotheology'.[13] Without entering into a full discussion of this much-debated term, part of what he means by this is that, in the Western tradition, both theology and philosophy have identified the God of religious faith and worship (the highest being) with the ultimate cause of all that exists (the first cause or being as such). Religious meaning, in other words, has been said by Christian theology to be grounded in knowledge of Being-Itself – although, as he also acknowledges, this can be, and has been, formulated in a variety of ways, and he lists *Physis*, *Logos*, *Hen*, *Idea*, *Energeia*, substantiality, objectivity, subjectivity, will, will-to-power, will-to-will (which last, as his own lectures show, refers precisely to the position of the later Schelling). But it would seem that, in these terms, Tillich's adoption of Being-Itself as the start and end point of his theological system marks him out as a prime exponent of ontotheology. Now, as Heidegger himself acknowledges, this is not some kind of commonplace error and may even be an unavoidable illusion of thought, but these comments do force us to ask whether Tillich has really done justice to the element of difference that the temporality of human life and thought involve and whether, in the end, his idea of God as Being-Itself can, in fact, serve the religious interest he attaches to it. These questions are further radicalized if we take seriously the French philosopher Jacques Derrida's principle of deconstruction, according to which the other basic claim of any system of identity will also inevitably fail, namely, the claim that we can formulate propositions that are stripped of all ambiguity and that achieve a full and adequate univocity.

DOI: 10.1057/9781137454478.0005

On the contrary, Derrida wrote, to some extent following Heidegger but with a greater focus on the 'written' structure of language, every statement will, in the end, deconstruct itself and the play of *différance* (as he wrote it) perpetually undo the attempt to impose or articulate a unitary meaning.

But if this Heideggerian–Derridian insistence on difference has proved characteristic of so-called postmodern thought, does this then mean that Tillich's system is condemned to have a merely historical interest and falls short of addressing the intellectual issues of our time?[14] We will have to examine the system itself much more closely before we can give any definite answer to this question, but it is my working assumption that even if questions will, in the end, remain (which Tillich himself would surely have acknowledged as inevitable), Tillich nevertheless has a significant contribution to make to the debates engendered by our own religious situation – but just what part remains to be discovered.

Notes

1   In English, at least, there is some inconsistency as to whether 'Being' and 'Being-Itself' should have capitalized first letters. However, at the risk of reinforcing what some might see as the reification of the notion of being in Tillich's work, I am both capitalizing and hyphenating the expression, unless directly citing an alternative orthography. I do so to draw attention to the fact that, in Tillich's usage, this is a technical term, the relation of which to other senses of 'being' must, to some extent, be bracketed.

2   See Chapter 5 in this volume.

3   Exodus 3.14. This closely mirrors the medieval Latin translation *Ego sum qui sum*. This translation has been widely challenged in the twentieth century, and this challenge is itself both philological and connected with the critique of ontology. See the discussion in my *God and Being: An Enquiry* (Oxford: Oxford University Press, 2011), pp. 19–21.

4   I should emphasize that I am paraphrasing the German Idealists' view of medieval philosophy, rather than adjudicating on whether they had got it right!

5   This was for what was called a 'Licentiate' in Theology, roughly equivalent to an MA thesis.

6   It should be stressed that it is not my intention here to discuss whether Tillich's interpretation of Schelling was 'correct', but merely to show how the dissertation can be used to illuminate his own subsequent development.

7   It should be acknowledged at the outset that many find Schelling even more confusing than Tillich. However, whilst admitting that some care and patience

may be needed in what follows, my hope is that it will help us to a larger view of what we might call the theologizing of philosophy in Tillich's own system and therefore to a better sense of what, in this case, the expression 'philosophical theology' might mean.

8   The view that Tillich derived his existentialism from Heidegger has been widely propagated and is still encountered in the secondary literature. But although Tillich would become aware of and responsive to Heidegger, Heidegger was not, in my view, a significant source for his own thinking. That there are, nevertheless, commonalities is undeniable, but this is in large part due to the fact that they are both negotiating the common heritage of German Idealism and its leading critics. At the same time, there are also striking differences, some of which we shall return to later in this chapter.

9   This might seem to bring Schelling into a certain proximity to the medieval philosophers' conception of God as *actus purus* [pure act]. However, it is not clear that the two conceptions can or should be immediately conflated.

10 This is the theme of Handel's oratorio 'The Triumph of Time' and of a number of other Renaissance and Baroque works of art and literature.

11 M. Heidegger, *Being and Time*, trans. E. Robinson and J. Macquarrie (Oxford: Blackwell, 1962), p. 19.

12 See M. Heidegger, *Identity and Difference*, trans. Joan Stambaugh ([Dual language edition] New York: Harper and Row, 1969).

13 See Heidegger, 'The Onto-theo-logical Constitution of Metaphysics' in idem, *Identity and Difference*, pp. 42–74.

14 A similar question is addressed in the article by John Thatamanil, 'Tillich and the Postmodern' in Russell Re Manning (ed.), *The Cambridge Companion to Paul Tillich* (Cambridge: Cambridge University Press, 2009), pp. 208–322. Charles E. Winquist has also offered significant reflections on Tillich and postmodern philosophy and theology, for example, in his *The Surface of the Deep* (Aurora CO: Davies, 2003), chapters 15 and 16, pp. 215–32. Although I shall arrive at my conclusion by a somewhat different route, I, like them, will offer qualified support for the view that Tillich's position has not been simply superseded by the postmodern critique of metaphysics. Perhaps Winquist's summing up catches the necessary combination of caution and approval: 'Tillich's God beyond God may be read as the modest avowal that our courage does not come from the nothingness of disbelief but from the concreteness of our innermost pathos to believe, in the shimmer, if no more than that, of a possible intimacy with being' (op. cit., p. 232). Another retrieval of Tillich in the postmodern context may be discernible in recent work by John D. Caputo. See John D. Caputo, *The Insistence of God: A Theology of Perhaps* (Bloomington: Indian University Press, 2013). Caputo sees Tillich as playing a pivotal role in the emergence of postmodern theology in the USA.

DOI: 10.1057/9781137454478.0005

2
Revolution

Abstract: *After Germany's military and political collapse at the end of the First World War, Tillich embraced socialism in a form close to that of the Marxist utopianism of Ernst Bloch. Opposing the view of 'scientific socialism' that socialism would arrive as a result of inevitable historical progress, Tillich believed it would result from a response to a prophetic vision of the future. This meant appealing to the non-alienated core of workers' existential experience. It also meant recognizing and confronting the demonic powers manifest in such phenomena as Nazism. When and how to respond becomes a question of recognizing the kairos, the right time, in the sense of the New Testament's 'fulness of time'.*

Pattison, George. *Paul Tillich's Philosophical Theology: A Fifty-Year Reappraisal.* Basingstoke: Palgrave Macmillan, 2015. DOI: 10.1057/9781137454478.0006.

DOI: 10.1057/9781137454478.0006

Living the end

In his exposition of Schelling's system, Tillich had already noted that the manifestation of the divine life in history could not be conceived of as a simple unfolding in time of what is eternally complete in the inner life of God. Given the nature of historical existence, such a manifestation would need to encounter and overcome what is contrary to the divine will in time and history, thereby revealing itself as the struggle against what-ought-not-to-be or, in theological terms, the struggle against sin and separation from God. Already prior to First World War, then, Tillich had identified the challenge that history posed to any philosophy of identity, but his experience of the war would further – and radically – deepen his sense of the tension between such a philosophy and the existential situation of fallen humanity.

Tillich volunteered for military service as an army chaplain on 1 October 1914. In the years that followed he participated in some of the most catastrophic battles of the war, notably the battle of Verdun in which a total of nearly 300,000 soldiers were killed and possibly up to a million wounded. His experiences led to an attack of what would today be called post-traumatic stress disorder, although he subsequently returned to the Front and, in the course of his war service, was awarded the Iron Cross First Class for valour.

Unsurprisingly, what he lived through in this time had a massive and even decisive impact on his thought. In the first instance, as he put it in one of his sermons, the war meant a new revelation of the power of death. 'The lid was torn off' the pre-war attempt to ignore the reality of death and, instead, 'The picture of Death appeared, unveiled, in a thousand forms. As in the late Middle Ages the figure of Death appeared in pictures and poetry, and the Dance of Death with every living being was painted and sung, so our generation – the generation of world wars, revolutions, and mass migrations – rediscovered the reality of death' (NB, 171). Or, as he wrote to one correspondent at home, 'I am an utter eschatologist – not that I have childish fantasies of the death of the world, but rather that I am experiencing the actual death of this our time. I preach almost exclusively "the end" ...'[1] The war was not just, literally, the end for thousands upon thousands of young lives but, as Tillich here suggests, it was also the end of a certain social order.

Like many of his contemporaries on all sides, Tillich had gone to war believing in the justice of the German cause and his early war sermons

DOI: 10.1057/9781137454478.0006

called on soldiers to be proud to serve their Kaiser.[2] By the end of the war, however, things were looking very different. The Kaiser himself abdicated and went into exile and the German Empire collapsed. Germany experienced a series of civil conflicts between communist groups and right-wing militias and, in this political maelstrom, Tillich was drawn, decisively, to the left. Although he long abstained from joining any political party, he was ready to vote for the Marxist Independent Social Democratic Party and his statements on behalf of 'religious socialism' – a broad term for a variety of Christian socialists – would draw criticism from Church authorities. Through the early 1920s he was also a participant in what was called the 'Kairos Group', a discussion group of left-oriented Christian and Jewish intellectuals.

In an early lecture on religious socialism, he argued that whilst Christianity could never identify itself absolutely with any one social group or movement, it only ever became a power in history by making concrete social commitments. In fact, it had always done this, as the Churches' identification in previous ages with, for example, feudalism, capitalism, and nationalism witnessed. Nevertheless, the normative force of Jesus ethic of love meant that it would always have greater internal affinity with some social movements than others and, Tillich stated, 'I am convinced that in our contemporary moment it must step out against the capitalist and militarist social order in which we stand and of which the ultimate logic was revealed in the World War' (GW2, 14). The socialist vision of community was fundamentally closer to the ideal of Christian love than the egoism of capitalist and nationalist world views and did not necessarily mean limiting human aspirations to narrow this-worldliness (GW2, 15–16). Marxism itself should not be accused of simple materialism, but, if properly understood, it points to the interdependence of the economic base and the spiritual superstructure of cultural life rather than the simple reduction of the latter to the former (GW2, 16). The actual opposition of many socialist leaders to the Church – including their embrace of atheism – was itself a response to the particular alignment of the Churches and the bourgeois social order characterizing the pre-war situation. Nor, despite Lutheranism's traditional political passivity, are all Christian Churches necessarily opposed to revolution, the idea of which finds support in both Calvinist and Catholic theologies (GW2, 18). In short, socialism presents the Church with a new ethical ideal (GW2, 19) and, since Tillich had started the talk by asserting that from now on ethical questions would take priority over traditional dogmatic

DOI: 10.1057/9781137454478.0006

issues (GW2, 13), a positive reaction to socialism was clearly going to be essential to the Church proving itself capable of future life (GW2, 20). His frustration with the actual response of the Church to this challenge can be seen from another essay in which he remarks that 'the depth of the gulf between the Churches and the mass of those who have found a new meaning to life in their Communist and Marxist faith has been chiefly caused by the attitude of the Churches' (GW10, 146).

The early lecture represents a collection of views from which Tillich would never basically retreat, although (as we shall see) other questions would later come to displace or overshadow the socialist challenge. Although never a political activist, Tillich's identification with the left, reinforced by his close association from 1929 onwards with the philosophers of the future Frankfurt School, notably Max Horkheimer, Karl Mannheim, and Theodor Adorno, resulted in his being amongst the first wave of academics suspended by the Nazi government in April 1933. His most political book, *The Socialist Decision*, published shortly beforehand, was amongst the works publicly burned in Frankfurt in May 1933. By the end of the year, Tillich and his wife had left for what would prove to be permanent exile in America.

What is important for us, however, is to see how these events were reflected in and impacted on Tillich's philosophical theology. I have suggested that there is an essential continuity in Tillich's thought from the time of the early work on Schelling through to his *Systematic Theology*. But continuity does not mean uniformity, and both the war and the subsequent decade and a half of social upheaval would do much to shape the particular concrete form his thought would take. If the Schelling dissertation already acknowledged the difficulty of incorporating history into a system of identity, the lived experience of 'the end' would find expression in themes that, if not new, were newly emphasized, notably the concepts of the demonic and the *Kairos*. We shall shortly return to both of these key terms, but first, I shall examine more closely how Tillich conceived of religious socialism and how his own thought was, in this period, religiously socialist. Fully to explore all that this involved would involve examining not only its theological aspect but also its complex critical cross-references to various currents of inter-war socialist thought in Germany. These were not only theoretical, but also reflected and reacted upon the developing political situation. In neglecting this aspect of Tillich's context, I acknowledge the risk of doing injustice to the full complexity of his religious socialism. Nevertheless, if we are to maintain

DOI: 10.1057/9781137454478.0006

our focus on Tillich's philosophical theology, some such abstraction is necessary if, in a larger perspective, regrettable.[3]

Religious socialism

The conventional Lutheranism of Tillich's upbringing had seen social problems as resolvable through personal relationships and Christian charity and was opposed to what it perceived as the cold impersonal welfare distributed by socialist legislation. After his socialist awakening, however, Tillich recognized that such Christian charity was incapable of addressing the real situation of mass deprivation in cities such as Berlin and that it was less 'a proof of love' and more 'a sign of injustice' (GW2, 32).

Crucially, what Tillich proposes under the rubric of 'religious socialism' is not simply a pragmatic recommendation that Churches and socialist parties should work together for the good of the poor but what he calls a 'dialectical' or 'dynamic' approach in which both religious and political elements allow themselves to be reshaped in striving for a future point of unity that is not yet given. If that meant leaving behind the current leaderships of both Churches and socialist parties, then so be it, he says (GW2, 33). The unlikelihood of either leaderships or adherents of either Christianity or socialism setting out in search of such an unknown point of unity is, of course, immediately apparent and it is easy enough to portray Tillich's religious socialism as utopian. In fact, he himself was under no illusions as to the imminent realization of his socialist hopes. On the contrary, it was an important element in his criticism of some current versions of socialism that they seemed to envisage the real possibility of bringing about a rational and harmonious social order within history. Theologically, he saw this as a case of 'Pelagian' optimism, which did not recognize the reality of the 'sin, cupidity, the will to power, the unconscious urge' that drove human beings to irrational acts of violence (IH, 56) such that 'the realization of the Kingdom of Justice and Peace within this existence is impossible. The Kingdom of God can never become an immanent reality, and the absolute can never be realized in space and time. Every utopianism must end with a metaphysical disappointment' (IH, 56). Admittedly, these words were written shortly after his emigration and in a time that seemed to witness the triumph of Nazism, yet they reflect what had been a consistent element in his thought – and, again, they are consistent with the basic positioning of the Schelling

DOI: 10.1057/9781137454478.0006

thesis, since the divine is only ever fully realized in its own eternal life, never in the sphere of historical becoming in which its appearance must always be partial or, at best, paradoxical.

Yet, if utopian hopes about realizing the Kingdom of God in history are erroneous, we should not just brush aside all suggestions for social change. This is the perennial tactic of bourgeois mediocrity and complacency. But if utopia is impossible, this doesn't rule out what Tillich affirms as 'the spirit of utopia', endorsing the Marxist utopianism of Ernst Bloch.[4] 'The beyond-ness of utopia is humanity stretching itself beyond its actual situation,' he writes. 'But this self-stretching is of his being. It is the adequate expression of an unrestful being and is thus the opposite of ideology ... The utopist knows that his ideas are not real – but he believes that they are becoming real. The typical ideologue does not know this. He supposes that he comprehends his being in his thoughts' (GW12, 257).

Three different attitudes seem to be in play here. In the first, which Tillich calls the attitude of the ideologue, the present social order is seen to reflect the reality of human nature. In metaphysical terms, this relates back to the idea of truth as the correspondence of what is in the mind (*mens*), that is, the idea, with what really is, the thing itself (*res*). The epitome of this view is Hegel's often-cited (though equally often misapplied) saying that 'the real is the rational and the rational is the real'. The second is the attitude of the misguided kind of utopist, who recognizes that there are manifold human possibilities that the present world-order suppresses but who also believes that in some historical future this will change and a social order will be inaugurated in which all human possibilities will be fulfilled. Like the ideologue, this kind of utopist also holds to the metaphysical principle of the adequation of idea and thing and regards their current separation as merely temporary and remediable. In this sense, then, there is only a relative difference between the bourgeois realist and the utopian leftist since both hold to the same basic view of truth. Both are, in effect, practitioners of the principle of identity. A second type of utopist, however, knows that idea and reality will never coincide and, precisely for that reason, concludes that we should therefore never settle for reality as it is. The world will never be brought into entire harmony with our ideals, but this doesn't mean we should give up trying to make it more ideal than it now is. This kind of utopist exemplifies a break with the metaphysical conception of truth as the adequation of idea and reality and, instead, finds truth in what a later

DOI: 10.1057/9781137454478.0006

philosopher would call 'the ethical demand' and which Tillich refers to as 'expectation'. At the same time, Tillich resists seeing this in terms of a simple moralism, since the demand can only ever be effective if its circumstances are such that it can be acted upon.[5] What matters is the right dialectical relationship between the two aspects.

In *The Socialist Decision*, Tillich articulates the metaphysical issue as the difference between a logic of essences and a logic of dynamic concepts or principles. Talk of the essence of history (or, for example, the essence of democracy or nationhood) actually abstracts from the living, changing reality of history itself, which is a reality that can never be captured in a simple, timeless definition as to what 'history' (or 'democracy' or 'nationhood') *is*. Yet, as Tillich comments, 'we cannot dispense with summarizing characterizations when we are dealing with a coherent movement' (SD, 9). In other words, we cannot help but generalize, but the way to do so is not by attempting some kind of static definition, as essentialist discourse does. 'In place of the concept of essence, which is derived from the knowledge of nature,' Tillich writes, 'we must introduce a dynamic concept, in accordance with the character of history. A concept is dynamic if it contains the possibility of making understandable new and unexpected realizations of a historical origin' (SD, 9).[6] Seeing religious socialism as just such a 'principle', he adds that its defining symbol is 'expectation'. 'Expectation' he says,

> is tension with a forward aim. Expectation directs itself towards what is not now, but shall be, towards something unconditionally new that has never been but is in the making... History drives forward from every present into the future. History is tension towards that which is to come; concretely towards the new order of things. The prophet awaits it; socialism strains towards it, regardless of how this straining may be expressed rationally. (SD, 102)

In these terms, then, socialism is not an 'idea' and offers neither a theory of historical progress nor a blueprint for a reformed society. The only way really to know 'what' socialism is, is actually to engage in the struggle to bring it about. The 'expectation' that characterizes socialist hope is not a mere passive 'waiting' but 'Expectation includes action. Only an expectation that evokes action is genuine' (SD, 105). But this also means that expectation relates itself to what is specific and concrete in the present moment – action always means doing just 'this' and not something else, deciding for some definite course of action and against whatever might be the alternative.

DOI: 10.1057/9781137454478.0006

This brings socialism's utopian expectation back down to the harsh reality of what Tillich calls 'the proletarian situation', that is, the actual repression suffered by the working class. 'The needs of man, of a sociologically homogenous mass of men tear away the ideological mask. They provide the criterion for distinguishing what is real from what is merely ideological. Anything that cannot rescue the proletariat from the perversion of existence in the capitalistic order is rejected' (PE, 247). This in turn means that religious socialism has to accept the reality of class struggle, since class struggle is the inevitable result of the free market economics espoused by bourgeois liberalism:

> The free market is the manifestation of the conflict of interests, of the war of all against all, accepted as a principle, hence of an activity motivated always by the impulse to seek one's own interests at the expense of others ... the conflict is not the expression of individual arbitrariness or of chaotic anarchy but is necessarily bound up with the maintenance of the capitalist economic system and is the result of that system itself. (RS, 109–10)

It is consequently irrelevant to decry socialism's embrace of class struggle as manifesting simple class hatred or resentment and it is futile and irresponsible to judge acceptance of class struggle moralistically (GW2, 185). In other words, it is not a failure in charity when socialism calls its followers actively to oppose bourgeois ownership of the means of production and distribution: it is simply to act in the light of a realistic appraisal of what is needed to remove the affliction of proletarian existence. This affliction includes the chronic threat of unemployment, the provision of low-grade goods, housing, and education, exclusion from the enjoyment of cultural goods, and the fragmentation of supportive structures of community life. As society is transformed into a technicized mass, the individual becomes a mere cog in the machined, an atomized 'thing' – as in Marxist theories of reification or Habermas's analysis of the instrumentalization of social relationships.

But socialism itself is all too often prone to treat the worker and the mass simply as an object, namely, the object of agitation, and, as such, mere material for producing revolutionary cadres or maximally efficient economic units. But 'something that has become merely a thing no longer resists its being made into thing' and 'The reaction of the proletarian ... is the reaction of a real human being' (SD, 98). In the spirit of the 'humanist' element of Marx that was being discovered in this period, Marxism should neither be about identifying immutable laws of history (there aren't any), nor about perpetuating the bourgeois

DOI: 10.1057/9781137454478.0006

reduction of the proletariat to the status of mere instrumentality; it should be about recognizing and empowering the genuinely human impulse to resist dehumanization that is manifested in the working-class human being's resistance to bourgeois rule. In these terms, class struggle becomes an expression of the human search for meaning in the face of everything that seeks to suppress or destroy it; it represents the universal human struggle to achieve fullness of being in defiance of the threats of non-being and absurdity. In these terms the working-class struggle is no longer just a struggle for the improvement of a particular section of society, but 'Class-consciousness is the historically-conditioned expression of the consciousness of humanity' (GW2, 85). Again, everything hinges on getting the right dialectical dynamism since if the proletarian struggle has a genuinely universal human significance, this is only on the basis of taking the particular situation of the working class fully seriously: 'Socialism is the expression of the proletarian situation' (SD, 62).

Let's return to the theme of expectation. What, then, is 'expected' or 'demanded' when the working class is aroused to seek a future in which social relations are fully humanized? We have seen that this must be more than a merely historical utopia (which is never going to arrive anyway), so what, then, is it? It is, as we have already seen Tillich imply, something that, within history, is more than historical. It is the advent of something unconditioned within the conditions of historical change and, as such, what Tillich calls 'theonomy', that is, the law or rule (*nomos*) of God and which he defines as 'the unity of holy form and holy content in a concrete historical situation' (GW2, 94).[7] Noting but not dwelling on the use of the philosophical categories of form and content that are clearly more Schellingian than Marxist, we see, then, how Tillich comes to see the universal meaning of the working-class struggle as manifesting a movement that is profoundly religious in nature. Because it relates to the real material affliction of proletarian existence, this is a movement that is this-worldly and, in technical parlance, immanent. But because it is reaching out towards something unconditional, something that can never become fully realized in history, it is transcendent. And it is indivisibly both: 'Human expectation is always transcendent and immanent at the same time. More precisely, this opposition does not exist for expectation' (SD, 110). This can be seen in ideas such as the classless society, which, Tillich says, is 'just as much a transcendent symbol as an immanent fact. Better still, one should say that it is neither the one nor the other, but rather that it shows the continual movement back and forth, the fluctuation and oscillation of real life' (SD, 111).

In these terms, then, the Marxist view of history becomes an early case study for Tillich's method of correlating theological and non-theological symbols and concepts.[8] But it is not simply that, in this case, the Marxist symbol of the classless society can be correlated with the prophetic symbol of the Kingdom of God. In both cases we are dealing with dynamic symbols that are not objects of theoretical observation but that constitute a demand for commitment and action. Rather, as Tillich goes on to say in continuance of the last quoted comment, '*Both prophetic and socialist expectation are a witness of life to its fundamental openness. They are a protest of life against false concepts of transcendence that inevitably call forth, in opposition, false concepts of immanence*' (SD, 111). This is why *The Socialist Decision* is said by Tillich to be both a book *about* socialism 'its nature, its problems, its difficulties, and its coming form' (SD, xxxi) and a book that urges its readers to make a decision *for* socialism. Arising from and addressing a living situation that was in many key respects open and undecided at the time of writing, *The Socialist Decision* was not a theoretical treatise about socialism or about the relationship between socialism and Christianity but an attempt to think socialism and Christianity together in such a way as to help avert the catastrophe of National Socialism. That it failed in this key aim should not, however, count too strongly against the argument it mounts. After all, none of the other alternatives available at the time – including purely political and purely religious alternatives – succeeded either. The catastrophe occurred. No one stopped Nazism's accession to power and Tillich's critics didn't succeed any more than he did. Failure in this context doesn't therefore exclude the possibility of offering positive lessons to any contemporary or future Christian–Marxist dialogue.

But, again, this is not the main issue of this study and our question is more precisely about what Tillich's religious socialism reveals about his evolving philosophical theology. Especially important is how it shows Tillich deepening and broadening the challenge posed by real historical life to the model of identity-difference-reconciliation that he had developed in the thesis on Schelling. My argument is that although his religious socialist emphasis on the openness of actual historical life and on the demand to bring forth a new state of historical affairs might suggest a break with any system of identity, Tillich's thought, even in these apocalyptic years, shows a complex balancing of identity and difference, being and novelty. Postponing the question as to how far such a balance is really sustainable, I want now to look more closely at a group of symbolic concepts central to the philosophy of history involved in Tillich's religious socialism that deepens the theological background of his socialist agenda. These are myths of origin, the demonic, and the *kairos*.

Myths of origin

Ernst Bloch defined religion in terms of the etymology of the Latin *re-ligio* as binding back, that is, binding humanity back to its origins. In these terms, religion is at its heart about humanity's bonds to the primordial powers of cosmos, family, and society, about the worship of ancestors, about maintaining the old traditions, and doing as people have done since time immemorial. The gods are those who created the world 'in the beginning' and the primary burden of myth and ritual is therefore to remind us of how, long ago, before recorded time, all things came to pass, and to set out the laws that have ever since and will for evermore prescribe the course of human life.

Tillich, like Bloch, believed that crucial elements in Judaism and Christianity broke with this model. The prophetic vision looks not to the past but to the future, to the coming Kingdom of God, and it demands human action in order to bring this desired future about. In fact, many biblical scholars of Tillich's generation saw the story of the Hebrew Bible in just these terms as the prophetic struggle against forms of religion that tied people back to archaic powers, subordinating the future to the past, and thus subjecting human freedom to the dominion of natural or cosmic powers. The prophetic attack on idolatry is precisely an attack on religious forms that bind human freedom to the rhythms of natural powers. And it is just this that Tillich sees being repeated in his own time in the phenomenon of Nazism, with its stress on the primacy of soil, blood, and social cohesion. In a world view shaped by the powers of origin, time always circles back to its point of origin and this in turn means that, ultimately, human identity is defined in terms of space: we are the people who live in this land and who do as the law of our land demands. In ontological terms – and in a passage that might be turned critically against Tillich's own typical identification of God and Being-Itself – this means that 'being is holy ... [Being] is itself the truth and the

DOI: 10.1057/9781137454478.0006

norm. It determines both the form and the limits of its space. Ontology is rooted in the myth of origin; it is bound to space ... [it] is the final and most abstract version of the myth of origin' (SD, 18).⁹

The primacy of space (and therefore, by implication, ontology) is fundamentally challenged in prophetic religion that, turning things round 180 degrees, looks to the future rather than to the past as the decisive focus of divine action. In such innovation, prophetic religion breaks not only with the pagan nature cults of Canaan but also, indirectly, with the assumptions of early Greek philosophy. 'It confronts the power and impotence of being with justice, arising from the demand' – which, Tillich says, also 'becomes concrete in the "I-Thou" encounter' which requires 'that the "Thou" be given the same dignity as the "I"' (SD, 6). The prophetic defeat of the powers of origin is taken further by the Enlightenment, and modern ideals of maximizing the autonomy and self-direction of the individual indicate how far these powers have been weakened. Yet even in modernity they retain a psychological foothold in, for example, '*eros, fate*, and *death*', which remain resistant to rationalization (SD, 25). And in what Tillich calls 'political romanticism' we see the attempt to reinstate the rule of the ancient powers in the political order, whether these are figured in terms of blood and soil, religious hierarchy, or, in more revolutionary terms, in the apocalyptic imagery implicit in the Nazis' vision of a Third Reich – a third Kingdom, corresponding to aspects of Christian apocalyptic thought.¹⁰

The demonic

Focused as it is on the exigency of contemporary political life, Tillich does not give a lot of attention in *The Socialist Decision* to the category of the demonic, but it can be seen as a further aspect of the background to his analysis of the myths of origin and political romanticism. The fullest account of this concept is in the section on 'The Demonic' of *The Interpretation of History*, which was originally a self-standing essay, published in 1926, and therefore contemporary with his religious socialist thinking.

We shall say more in the next chapter on Tillich's view of art, but here too art provides the starting point for the analysis of the demonic, more specifically the Western encounter with what Tillich (doubtless to our minds unfortunately) calls 'the art of primitive people and Asiatics,

DOI: 10.1057/9781137454478.0006

embodied in statues of their Gods and fetishes, in the crafts, and dance masks' (IH, 77).[11] What interests him in this material is that it reveals 'depths of reality which had, to be sure, escaped our consciousness, but in subconscious strata had never ceased to determine our existence' (IH, 77). These images 'bear forms, human, animal, and plant, which we understand as such, recognizing their conformity to artistic laws. But with these organic forms are combined other elements which shatter our every conception of organic form'. Stressing that this is not due to any supposed 'primitive lack of development' or 'as a limitation of an aptitude for artistic form', Tillich describes these 'other elements' as destructively violating 'the organic coherence presented in nature', and mocking 'all natural proportion'. He continues: 'The organs of the will for power, such as hands, feet, teeth, eyes, and the organs of procreation, such as breasts, thighs, sex organs, are given a strength of expression which can mount to wild cruelty and orgiastic ecstasy' (IH, 78). But the fact that this occurs in works of art means that it is not to be written off as simply evidencing a lack of form. It is something more than any mere 'lack': it is the active contradiction of form and, as such, 'something contra-positive'. 'Only by denying, on principle, the esthetic qualities of a negro sculpture or a Shiva picture, could one escape this conclusion, i.e., by making classical esthetics absolute. Whoever cannot assent to this conclusion, must admit that human art reveals to us the actuality of that which is positively contrary to form, the demonic' (IH, 79).

What is revealed in such 'primitive' art finds manifold (Tillich says 'innumerable') expressions in the history of religion, in 'orgiastic phallus cults', 'ritual prostitution', 'laceration-myths and orgies', 'blood sacrifice to the god of earth who devours life in order to create life', 'war gods', Moloch, and, in a more contemporary form, 'the demonic will to power of the sacred institution' revealed in Dostoevsky's 'Grand Inquisitor' (IH, 79–80).[12] All such phenomena constitute the domain of the demonic.

But behind (as it were) the demonic is another power, which Tillich calls 'the Satanic'. This latter is the power of destruction without creation and which, as he points out, is a contradiction in terms since, unlike the demonic, the Satanic 'has no actual existence' because 'in order to have existence, it would have to be able to take on form, i.e., to contain an element of creation' (IH, 80). By isolating destruction from creation and attempting to make it into an independent principle, the Satanic, which 'ontologically speaking... is the negative principle contained in the demonic' (IH, 81), condemns itself to non-existence. What is represented

DOI: 10.1057/9781137454478.0006

as Satanic can only acquire form by means of what contains or manifests the power of creation – and this is precisely what is demonic, that is, 'the unity of form-creating and form-destroying strength' (IH, 81). The mere dissipation or decline of a given phenomenon (e.g. an organic body or a beneficent social institution) is not in itself the result of 'demonry' if it is simply the outcome of a progressive loss of being. We can only speak of a 'demonic' attack on what is good when there is real creative energy on the part of the 'demon'. But the power that the demon has is, on closer analysis, a power rooted in the depth of the phenomenon itself, it is '"another thing," which is still no other thing, but a depth in the things, [which] is not rational, i.e., demonstrable from the interrelation of things with the world... but a quality of things which reveals – or conceals – a view into its depths' (IH, 83).

This is – it cannot be anything but – opaque. What is Tillich saying here?

The point, I think, is this. As in Boehme's cosmology (incorporated, as we saw, into Schelling's system), there is no ultimate ground or reason to existence or being. The *Urgrund* or primordial ground of all things is an *Ungrund*, a non-ground, that, as Tillich glosses it here, is to be construed as 'an active inexhaustibility, i.e., as the "consuming fire," that becomes a real abyss for every form' (IH, 84). In other words, there is no final 'what' or essence that makes things be what they are: they are what they are only by virtue of a dynamic process of coming into existence. But the very energy that drives things to come into existence and to find form simultaneously imperils both existence and form. Perhaps – although this is not an example Tillich specifically uses – we might think of the typical 'hell-raiser' personality; that is, someone whose exceptional zest for life hurls them into a sequence of misadventures and addictions that are likely to end by destroying the life they seem so eager to affirm and are so full of. And if Tillich doesn't use this particular example, he does emphasize that a demonic personality is the most extreme manifestation of the demonic since the 'form' of personality is precisely connected to reason and freedom, whereas demonic personalities are people whose freedom is possessed by a power they seem unable to control or direct – although it is, paradoxically, the power of their 'own subconscious. As in all of its manifestations, the power of the demonic flows from the energy of its victims' own original *Urgrund*, impelling them to ecstatic or frenzied action they cannot explain or control. This may raise them to heights of unexpected creativity, but, Tillich suggests, it will end with purely destructive eruptions of energy. Yet the elements of creativity and consciousness mean that the demonic is not simply identifiable with the unconscious; it points to a power beyond dualism and, in doing so, has a certain analogy to the religious, for example, to the experience of divine grace as helping us to do or to be what we could not do on our own.

In turning to the specific forms of the demonic in his own time, Tillich identifies two 'demonries' that, as he puts it, 'surpass all the others in significance and symbolic force and shape the face of our times' (IH, 119). These are two phenomena that directly relate to the issue of religious socialism, namely free market economics and nationalism. On the basis of what we have already heard of Tillich's critique of political romanticism, the second of these is scarcely surprising, but why free market economics should be a primary example of the demonic is less immediately obvious. After all, isn't this precisely a phenomenon in which we see the highest development of scientific economics, and the constant transformation of human life styles through constant technical innovation? What could all this have in common with the atavistic forces revealed in romantic attachments to the powers of origin?

Tillich is himself attentive to the achievement of free market capitalism. 'Autonomous economics', he writes, 'with the help of the means technical science has placed at its disposal, is the most successful form of production of goods which has ever existed. The mechanism of the free market is the most artful machined for the equalization of supply and demand, as well as for the constant increase of needs and satisfaction of needs, which can be conceived' (IH, 119). Why, then, is it demonic? Essentially, Tillich's suggestion seems to be that although it is a power that uses human ingenuity and intelligence, it cannot ever be fully controlled by those who are its agents. It is fundamentally beyond control, a fact which becomes manifest in the moments of crisis to which the system is inherently exposed. We have already seen how Tillich portrays the proletarian situation as especially exposed to the negative impacts of such crises and how the affliction of the working classes becomes a demand for transformative social action.

The problem is not the immorality of, for example, bankers or financiers. Central to the point of seeing the market as a form of the demonic is that it reveals a power greater than that of individual actions or choices. It is not as if the market is an efficient machine that is from time to time thrown off balance by the malpractice of a few exceptionally voracious and immoral individuals. The instability is in the system itself. In this

DOI: 10.1057/9781137454478.0006

perspective, then, Tillich would presumably not have been surprised by now familiar images of frantic Wall Street traders desperately shouting into their headsets and wildly gesturing with their arms to battle off an invisible yet impending stock market crash, since these are images that seem to show human beings who are, literally, out of themselves, gripped by powers they suddenly recognize to be beyond their control. It is the situation of Faust, in the moment when he realizes for the first time the price that he will now have to pay for the promised years of achievement and pleasure. This is why it is 'demonic'.

Crucial to Tillich's religious socialism is the fusion of the demonry of free market capitalism with the other great contemporary form of the demonic: nationalism. In the past, nationalism had resources to offer some resistance to the unrestricted sway of the markets (and, in our own day, it is clear that many are turning to nationalism with just this hope). But by the early twentieth century, nationalism had, in effect, become subordinated to capitalism and, in this role, was able to provide capitalism with the kinds of energies that flowed from the powers of origin – loyalty to kith and kin, to people, race, and nation. 'Thus the social demonry of the present is revealed in its duality, in its immense supporting and destructive strength. Shattered for a moment, it is at present on the point of re-establishing itself, in order better to sustain and – better to destroy' (IH, 121).

Although National Socialism was still only a marginal political force at the time when Tillich wrote these words, its subsequent triumph would seem perfectly to have fitted his prognosis. At the same time, this analysis makes clear why Tillich rejected the kind of socialism to which the mainstream of the Social Democratic Party adhered and according to which socialism would more or less inevitably come to pass as a result of the gradual and progressive rationalization of social and economic relationships. The problems of capitalism cannot be solved by rational adjustments. As Tillich puts it, 'Demonry breaks down only before divinity, the possessed state before the state of grace, the destructive before redeeming fate' (IH, 122). But this also means that whilst the only appropriate response to historical manifestations of demonic power is to oppose power to power, there can be no final overcoming of the demonic within history. It is only in relation to the eternal, Tillich concludes, that we can speak of the demonic as finally and definitively overcome. And, again, the limitations of all possible social progress come into view: no future society will ever be able to entirely eliminate the possibility of one

DOI: 10.1057/9781137454478.0006

element within society rising up and taking demonic possession of the rest. In fact, given the proximity of the demonic to the dynamic energy of human creativity, this will not only remain possible but is also likely.

Kairos

All of this seems to offer little by way of help in thinking strategically about how to deal with a demonic phenomenon such as the rise of Nazism. If, having recognized its demonic character, we feel called to act against it, how are we to know when or how to act? If the Social Democrats' belief in inevitable progress led to a kind of complacent passivity that judged the resurgence of ultra-nationalism to be only a temporary blip on the inevitable path to socialism, Tillich's analysis of it as a kind of demonry that could only fully be overcome in eternity might, for quite opposite reasons, also lead to the conclusion that there was little if anything that could actually be done about it at the level of political action. Yet we have seen that the 'expectation' proclaimed in *The Socialist Decision* was seen by Tillich as inseparable from a call to action. But if there can be no rational criteria sufficient to provide an effective plan of action against a truly demonic phenomenon, does this mean that Tillich's socialism results in a kind of decisionism, that is, a political view that sees decision and action as, so to speak, self-validating, finding the sole justification for acting in such and such a way and at such and such a moment in the action itself. Referring to what he calls 'the younger circle' of the *Neue Blätter für den Sozialismus* (*New Sheets for Socialism*), a journal that he himself helped set up, Tillich spoke of them as being led 'toward a voluntaristic, ethical socialism that at the same time better satisfied its impulse for "socialist action"'(SD, xxxiv).

But if the category of the demonic indicates how Tillich's interpretation of history rejects any purely rationalistic optimism, the call to action is not left devoid of all content. Not any action, any where, any time, solely for action's sake will do. There is a right time to act and this 'right time' becomes a key element in Tillich's thought, often expressed by the term *kairos*. The word itself derives from the New Testament, meaning the right time or the moment that is the fullness of time, as when Jesus is described coming into Galilee and preaching 'The time (*ho kairos*) is fulfilled [or, in older translations 'at hand']: the Kingdom of God is upon you' (Mk 1.15). The idea is also taken up in the teaching that Christ's

DOI: 10.1057/9781137454478.0006

own coming occurred 'in the fullness of time' (Col 1.10). In both cases it suggests that God's purposes cannot be fulfilled at just any time, but there is a right time, a time that is prepared for in a particular sequence of historical events. Whereas in the Platonic scheme truth is equally near and equally far from human beings at all times, the biblical narrative suggests that God's relation to human beings is, as it were, 'timed'. Particular moments of time have particular significance and provide the unique occasion for a specific encounter with or response to the divine purpose – and it is in this sense also that Jesus can speak of Jerusalem not recognizing the 'hour of its visitation' (Lk 19.44). Time qualified in this way is no longer simply *chronos*, time measured by the movement of celestial bodies or the ticking of a clock (as in 'chronology' or 'chronometer'), but time for decision and action.

The term had, in fact, become current in philosophy and theology through the influence of Kierkegaard, who introduced it in opposition to idealist philosophy's attempt to survey human life as if *sub specie aeternitatis*, that is, from an eternal view point that gives no special privilege to any one moment of time over any other – all times, from such a view point, are equally near to (and equally far from) God.[13] Following Kierkegaard, it had been further popularized by Heidegger and other philosophers of existence as well as by the theology of crisis, represented by Karl Barth and others. As in Kierkegaard, much was made of the Danish/German connotations of the term used to translate *kairos*: *Øjeblikket* or *Augenblick*, literally, the glance or 'twinkling' of an eye, which allows us to translate Heidegger's and Tillich's use of *Augenblick* as 'moment of vision'. This is important because it indicates that the *kairos* is not just a kind of time but a kind of time involving a spontaneous vision of how things are and what needs to be done. In other words, the action that becomes appropriate in such a moment of vision is not blind action for action's sake, as in both left-wing and right-wing versions of decisionism, but action that incorporates a definite perception or understanding of what is at issue. In religious socialism, for example, it is the motivating power of the demand for a classless society or of the prophetic vision of the coming Kingdom of God. But because action will only be effective when it is in accordance with the *kairos*, it must also take into account the whole ensemble of circumstances with which it has to deal, such as is provided by the analysis of the affliction of the proletarian situation and why this cannot be remedied by capitalism itself. The moment of vision and the moment of decision must come together in and at 'the right time'.

DOI: 10.1057/9781137454478.0006

Although the biblical idea of time as leading towards a decisive *kairos* is therefore opposed to the philosophical pursuit of timeless truths, it is not devoid of what Tillich calls *logos*: the word or reason that explains the aim and purpose of decisive action. And, he argues, the philosophers' privileging of the timeless *logos* is, in reality, only one possibility. As German philosophy from Hegel has realized, the *logos* itself has a historical character: reason has a history. But, as Schelling had already realized, this means that our human experience of *logos* has a fateful character. The reason why I am living is not a reason I can grasp equally well at just any time (as I can, in principle, grasp the theory of Pythagoras equally well at any time of my life). Rather, the reason why I am living will in all likelihood only reveal itself to me – if at all – in relation to a particular and unrepeatable set of circumstances. It is the revelation of my destiny and what I am called upon to be and to do in my life. So too with regard to the historical life of human communities. Not everything is equally possible at any time. Both understanding and action are a matter of destiny. But this is, once more, to bring us back to the essentially dialectical nature of Tillich's key concepts. Where one kind of philosopher will simply oppose *logos* to *kairos*, arguing that for truth to be true it must be susceptible of being equally true at all times and in all places, and where one kind of decisionist will simply spurn all talk of *logos*, Tillich sees knowledge and fate or destiny as interrelated. 'Dialectics is the attempt to comprehend the fate of the idea from our Kairos, from the fate of our period. [But] because this attempt recognizes itself as fate, it does not transcend fate but remains within it' (IH, 169).

The struggle for political action on behalf of what ought to be against the hegemony of a given established order and the struggle to understand the meaning of this struggle itself are both carried on within time, within history, and are therefore subject to the rise and fall of historical time. And perhaps, as Tillich would come to think in the post-war period and in the light of the advent of the Cold War, this might mean accepting that there can also be times of waiting, times devoid of *kairos*, when any decisive or unqualified commitment or action would be for the wrong reason and in the wrong cause. This means accepting both an element of fate or destiny and the impossibility of any final or definitive realization of some envisaged utopian future. But if this seems to be leading us to a thoroughly dialectical and open-ended scenario in which everything is only ever provisional and only ever relative to everything else, oscillating backwards and forwards between contrary possibilities, we have

DOI: 10.1057/9781137454478.0006

to remind ourselves that Tillich did, nevertheless, affirm the power of what he variously called the absolute, the unconditioned, the eternal, Being-Itself – God. But how, in time and in the face of such historical catastrophes as the Battle of Verdun, the rise of Nazism, or the Cold War can we also affirm the triumph of what is more than time? How can we go on hoping, when our best hopes for ourselves and our society are repeatedly dashed by bitter historical experience? Where – or perhaps more accurately, when – in history does the power of what is more than historical ever become truly manifest? Tillich's answer to this question is above all to be found in his doctrine of Christ, and it is therefore to his Christology that, in the following chapter, we now turn.

Notes

1 Wilhelm and Marion Pauck, *Paul Tillich: His Life and Thought, Volume 1: Life* (London: Collins, 1977), p. 51.

2 His army sermons have now been published in German, but are not yet available in English.

3 A useful discussion of Tillich's religious socialism and, especially, its debated relation to the Frankfurt School of Critical Theory can be found in Gary M. Simpson, *Critical Social Theory: Prophetic Reason, Civil Society, and Christian Imagination* (Minneapolis: Fortress Press, 2002), chapter 2, pp. 27–52.

4 On similarities and differences in Bloch's and Tillich's approaches see my *Eternal God/Saving Time* (Oxford: Oxford University Press, 2015), chapter 6 'The Call to Utopia', pp. 173–211.

5 We shall explore more of what this could mean in connection with the idea of the *kairos*.

6 Again, the analogy with the Schellingian 'potencies' seems unmissable.

7 We shall return to the meaning of theonomy in the next chapter.

8 For further discussion of the method of correlation see Chapter 5 in this book.

9 The tension between ontology and hope in Tillich and Bloch is dealt with more fully in my *Eternal God/Saving Time*.

10 Where this differs from the future orientation of genuinely prophetic concepts would seem to be that apocalyptic thought represents the future as essentially the return of a primordial age of plenitude and innocence, whereas prophetic thought is concerned with the concrete transformation of actual historical injustice. However, it might be conceded that it is not always going to be obvious in any given case of apocalyptic imagery (biblical or post-biblical) whether it is the mythical or the prophetic element that

DOI: 10.1057/9781137454478.0006

predominates and considerable interpretative tact might be needed to make the appropriate distinction.

11   Although his discussion will continue to reveal strongly Eurocentric assumptions, further consideration of his theory of art will show that his views should by no means be taken as constituting a simply negative judgement on this art or as implying that 'primitive' art is unknown in Western art. Indeed, it is precisely such comparable effects that Tillich especially seems to value in contemporary expressionism.

12   Tillich acknowledged Karl Barth's jibe that Tillich's work could be seen as a lifelong obsessive struggle against the Grand Inquisitor.

13   The idea plays an important role in *The Concept of Anxiety*, a work that also stressed other notions such as anxiety and the demonic that would be taken up by Tillich and others in the early twentieth century.

DOI: 10.1057/9781137454478.0006

3

Revelation

Abstract: *Tillich's understanding of art, shaped by contemporary German expressionism, provides an analogy and perhaps even an exemplification of what he means by religious revelation. However, the primary locus of such revelation – revelation of what he calls the New Being – is the revelation of the Christ. But, against the openness to the future of radical hope, this seems to tie revelation back both to a pre-given ontological structure and to the historical person of Jesus, believed in and proclaimed as the Christ. Appealing to the Kierkegaardian idea of paradox, Tillich nevertheless argues that it is possible to experience the eternal as revealed in temporal experience, thus providing a ground for existential hope.*

Pattison, George. *Paul Tillich's Philosophical Theology: A Fifty-Year Reappraisal*. Basingstoke, Palgrave Macmillan, 2015. DOI: 10.1057/9781137454478.0007.

Revelation in art

Although there is some evidence for Tillich's having had some interest in visual art prior to the First World War, it was only when he was on leave from the front line that he came to realize the potential *power* of art.[1] As he describes it, this realization came in the form of an overwhelming experience in the face of the painting *Madonna with Singing Angels*, in what was then called the Kaiser Friedrich Museum in Berlin. Later Tillich wrote of this experience:

> Gazing up at it, I felt a state approaching ecstasy. In the beauty of the painting there was beauty itself. It shone through the colors of the paint as the light of day shines through the stained-glass windows of a medieval Church. As I stood there, bathed in the beauty its painter had envisioned so long ago, something of the divine source of all things came through to me. I turned away shaken ... That moment has affected my whole life ... I compare it with what is usually called revelation in the language of religion. (AA, 230)

We shall shortly return to the question as to the analogy between this kind of experience and religious revelation, but this revelatory moment also marked the beginning of what would be an important sub-theme of Tillich's subsequent theological writing, namely, the meaning and significance of visual art for the interpretation of human existence. In fact, Tillich would be nearly unique amongst the leading Protestant theologians of his time in making space for visual art in his theological work. One of the characteristic features of the Protestant Reformation had been the rejection of the rich – and in Protestant eyes, excessive – visual culture of the late Middle Ages, a culture also connected with a focus on sacramental practice rather than biblical teaching.[2] In some cases (as in Britain) this involved the destruction of works of art on a massive scale. Lutheranism was generally more restrained, but, as Tillich himself would affirm on his own behalf, the typical Protestant view was that, in comparison with visual art or sacramental symbols, 'the word is the Spirit's ... ultimately more important medium' ST3, 132).[3] Nevertheless, despite this Protestant bias towards the word, Tillich would vastly extend modern Protestant theology's openness to visual art and to a wider sense of sacramental, that is, non-verbal communication, including, especially, dance. And if today 'the arts' are a recognized and expanding feature of theological education, this is in large part owing to Tillich's initiative, at least in the Protestant world.

DOI: 10.1057/9781137454478.0007

However, Tillich's engagement with art was also innovative in relation to conventional Catholic approaches. For whilst Catholicism had always affirmed the use of images in religious life, it had proved suspicious, not to say hostile, to the successive waves of modern art that, by the early twentieth century, had completely transformed the world of visual art. Tillich, however, expressly and especially affirmed the religious value of modern art, above all the expressionism inspired by Eduard Munch and Van Gogh and practiced by members of the 'Blue Rider' school. Later his passion would extend to the '*Neue Sachlichkeit*' ('new matter-of-factness') of Georg Grosz and Otto Dix and, in the 1950s, to Mark Rothko. Many of these works were regarded by many theologians as expressive of unbelief, nihilism, and a generally un-Christian view of the world. It also has to be said that they were works of a very different kind from the Botticelli painting that had so inspired Tillich's involvement with visual art.

At first, Tillich's approach to art was dovetailed into his socialist critique of existing society. In an early essay entitled 'Mass and Personality' he describes the different ways in which the human crowd has been represented artistically in different ages, coming down to the present. In the course of the essay, Tillich also draws a contrast between what he sees going on in French impressionism and German expressionism. The impressionists portray only the surface life of the modern urban crowd, seeing in it no more than a play of colours to be reproduced through displays of technical virtuosity that are entirely devoid of depth or critique. As such, it manifests the ideology of the French bourgeoisie and what he would elsewhere call its 'self-sufficient finitude' (RS, 86). Expressionism, by way of contrast, enters into the turbulent inner feeling that lies beneath the surface and, in doing so, moves beyond justifying the status quo to a new kind of metaphysical perception. It reveals society as desperately, and perhaps even despairingly, experiencing the collapse of an old order and discerns a longing for a future transformation of society from below. Although it would be fulfilled in a way that he would see as disastrous (i.e. the rise of Hitler), there is an uncannily prescient edge to his comment that the redeemer now being awaited 'cannot come from above. He must be born from the depth of the mass longing' (AA, 63). In any case, such art is art possessed of a 'revolutionary consciousness and revolutionary force' (AA, 87). Later, Tillich would extend this analysis of expressionism more generally to take in what he saw as an expressionist or expressive element in art of many different schools and ages. As such it is art that 'disrupts the naturally given appearance of things', revealing

DOI: 10.1057/9781137454478.0007

'the "dimension of depth" in the encountered reality, the ground and abyss in which everything is rooted' (AA, 123). This can also, he said, be correlated with 'the ecstatic-spiritual type of religious experience' (AA, 150). Examples might include El Greco or the kind of so-called primitive art discussed in the previous chapter.

The idea of expressionism is productive in Tillich's more narrowly philosophical and theological writings in two main ways. First, it is itself an example of revelation. Even if, in the first instance, what it reveals is precisely the demonic or the longing for redemption rather than redemption itself, it nevertheless leads us to those depths of existence in which religious questions first become real and urgent. Again, we might comment on how this illuminates his method of correlation, since even if expressionist art cannot of itself give a religious answer to the human question, it does nevertheless reveal that question in all its religious power. As he several times puts it, it reveals the cross, but not the resurrection. Theology is therefore obliged to pay attention to this *Miserere*, since its answers will only make sense to the extent that they are answers to questions that are really being asked – and this is precisely the central function of correlation. Resurrection is religiously meaningful only to those who have experienced the shadow of the cross.

But, second, expressionism serves theology by providing an analogy as to how we are to approach the gospel portrait of Jesus as the Christ. This is neither to be understood as an attempt at a realistic photograph, as debates about the 'historical Jesus' often assume, nor is it a mere vehicle for ideas about some ideal God-man, as in Hegelian views of the Christ-idea. Instead, it is to be 'an "expressionist" portrait' that expresses the painter's own 'profound participation in the reality and the meaning of his subject-matter' (ST2, 133). In other words, the revelation of God in Christ cannot be seen by focusing on the historical details of the life of Jesus not by trying to distil a certain ideal spiritual essence from it. Rather, it only becomes revelation in the full sense when it is revealed as answering the existential question of those human being whose lives have become focused on the all-embracing need for redemption.

Putting these two points together, we might say that, for Tillich, expressionist art is revelatory because, in the first instance, it reveals the abyssal questions that unsettle the very heart of human existence whether these take a societal or an individual form; but, second, it points us towards what is revelation in the full sense: the revelation of God as what Tillich would call 'the New Being', that is, God as the power to bring about the

DOI: 10.1057/9781137454478.0007

renewal and restoration of human beings' original identity with God, that is, with Being-Itself. In this way, such art reveals possibilities of meaning even in the most extreme situations of alienation and estrangement. And perhaps, by giving them artistic form, it is even able to offer a partial and preliminary conquest of the demonic powers that too often threaten to tear apart the fragile weave of human existence. Such revelations do not have to wait upon the transformation of human relationships in a future classless society (or, in religious terms, in the coming Kingdom of God) but constitute the revelation of meaning here and now, in the present.

Revelation, history, and being

All of this raises an important question about the relationship between present and future, or between what is and what is to come. For if, as the possibility of artistic revelation suggests, revelation can occur now, in the present, what scope or task is left for the God whose Kingdom is still to come? Won't the possibility of such a present revelation weaken the urge to act for the coming of a future utopian world – as revolutionaries would repeatedly complain about 'merely' artistic protests against the established powers?[4]

These reflections prompt a broader question that concerns the whole way in which Tillich conceives the relationship between history and ontology. In terms of his own religious socialism, we might put this question in terms of how a view of history that culminates in the fateful demand of the socialist decision can actually be accommodated within or alongside the kind of systematic account of identity-estrangement-reconciliation that we surveyed in Chapter 1. At one point we heard Tillich himself describing the prophetic struggle as a struggle against the atavistic gods of space and of cyclical time and asserting that '[o]ntology is rooted in the myth of origin; it is bound to space... [it] is the final and most abstract version of the myth of origin' (SD, 18). In this regard, Tillich might seem to be not so far from Emmanuel Lévinas, who would oppose the messianic claims of the divine demand for justice to any philosophical ontology that would, in his view, necessarily limit in advance the scope of what is possible for anything to be. But if that is so, then what are we to say of a system that itself insists on Being-Itself as the one non-symbolic divine name? Isn't Tillich's mature achievement itself an example – in theological terms, perhaps a supreme example – of

DOI: 10.1057/9781137454478.0007

theological ontology and a vindication of the ultimate triumph of identity over difference?

The question about the relation of history to ontology is sharpened if it is also claimed that the definitive form in which Being-Itself is revealed is an event of past history – as when revelation is eminently identified with the revelation of the New Being in Jesus as the Christ. Won't the combined force of the present tense of the divine being and the past tense of historical revelation more or less inevitably weaken or displace the future force of the socialist demand? Won't revelation necessarily trump revolution?

Although he was strongly opposed to any theological ontology, this seems to have been the conclusion of Karl Barth, the main representative amongst Tillich's contemporaries of a theology based solely on divine revelation. Commenting on Romans 13.1, where St Paul writes 'Let everyone be subject to the powers that be', Barth argued that the difference between the rebel and the established order was, theologically, only ever a relative difference. Asking his readers to suppose that the relationship between 'State, Church, Law, Society, &c., &c. – in their totality be: (a b c d)', what Barth called 'the Primal order of God' could be expressed by putting a minus sign outside the bracket in which these elements of the established order were contained, thus - (+a+b+c+d). But this is very different from the revolutionary's attempt to change the plus signs within the bracket s into minus signs, thus (−a −b−c−d). Nevertheless, the power of God is such that reinstating the minus sign outside the bracket – as in – (−a −b−c−d) – would mean that the minus signs inside the brackets are turned back into plus signs (since − (−a −b−c−d) = (+a+b+c+d). But if the arithmetic is confusing, Barth's verbal commentary makes the point clear enough: 'Revolution has, therefore, the effect of restoring the old after its downfall in a new and more powerful form .... To *be in subjection* .... [means] that men have encountered God, and are thereby compelled to leave the judgement to Him'.[5] Barth was himself a socialist but, as this passage makes it clear, he did not regard the decision for socialism as having ultimate religious significance in the way that Tillich argued for. The judgement is God's and solely God's and therefore every human political judgement is relative and corrigible.

Both ontology and revelation, it seems, are likely to undermine the urgency of any call to action in a fateful historical *kairos* and when, as in Tillich's system, *both* are simultaneously affirmed as integral to theological teaching, won't this undercut everything that religious socialism set out to achieve?

DOI: 10.1057/9781137454478.0007

One way of tackling this question is to see it less in terms of an internal contradiction in Tillich's thought and more as marking an actual shift away from 'the socialist decision' and towards a more consistently ontological approach. It is certainly the case that in the post-war period, Tillich's thought becomes less emphatically socialistic, and more focused on questions of art, existential philosophy, and depth psychology (although all of these were also present in his writings prior to the emigration). This is in part connected with his interpretation of the Cold War as inaugurating 'a time of waiting' and which, he said, was the 'special destiny' of that time (SF, 152). After all, the decisive breakthrough that he looked for in the *kairos* of 1933 didn't occur. Instead of making the socialist decision he demanded the German people chose Adolf Hitler and, albeit largely unawares, all the consequences that flowed from that choice. These consequences included the post-war order in which the political map came to be divided between a kind of totalitarian communism that Tillich had never supported and what he called the 'democratic conformism' that he encountered in America. But neither the one nor the other could, in his view, claim the right to constitute a new *kairos*. The only option was to wait in conscious recognition that we do *not* have any of the final answers. Tillich concludes the sermon as follows: 'Our time is a time of waiting; waiting is its special destiny. And every time is a time of waiting, waiting for the breaking in of eternity. All time runs forward. All time, both in history and in personal life, is expectation. Time itself is waiting, waiting not for another time, but for that which is eternal' (SF, 152). Certainly, there is some continuity with the views he had put forward in 1933. He still insists that time has the character of expectation. But this is no longer expectation directing us to act for the bringing about of the classless society as a historically concrete symbol and form of the Kingdom of God. It is waiting for the eternal rather than a call to *action*.

Paradox and new being

In connection with the shift from action to waiting, it seems that in Tillich's later thought the symbol of the Kingdom of God recedes in favour of the Christological symbol of the Incarnation. Also, the term '*kairos*' comes to have a more pronounced relation to the *kairos*, the fulfilled time, of the Incarnation, which, following Paul, he described as 'the moment of time in which God would send his Son. The moment which was selected to become the centre of history' (ST3, 394). If the 1926 essay on *kairos* and *logos* that was discussed in the previous chapter did not once specifically mention Christ or the Incarnation, the *Systematic Theology* makes it clear that this is, in fact, *the kairos* in an emphatic sense that both makes possible and gives meaning to all the other decisive moments of history. As Tillich now puts it 'The relation of the one *kairos* to the *kairoi* is the relation of the criterion to that which stands under the criterion and the relation of the source of power to that which is nourished by the source of power' (ST3, 395). But if history already has a 'centre' and a 'criterion' and if the 'source of power' of historical meaning has already appeared in history, then, once more, it seems that future-directed action is going to be proportionately reduced in significance. If believing that Jesus is the Christ, the Messiah, evokes the utopian prophetic symbol of the Messiah and his Messianic reign, Christian faith, unlike Jewish Messianism, holds, precisely, that the Messiah, *has come* and that all the fulfilment that is possible within historical time has occurred already in history, namely, in his manifestation. No greater fulfilment could, surely, come. It is in this way that he can be the centre of history. Tillich makes essentially the same point when he writes that 'In terms of the eschatological symbolism it can also be said that Christ is the end of existence. He is the end of existence lived in estrangement, conflicts, and self-destruction ... in him the New Being is present. His appearance is "realised eschatology" (Dodd) ... in so far as no other principle of fulfilment can be expected. In him has appeared what fulfilment qualitatively means' (ST2, 137). Of course, as Tillich acknowledges, 'In the sense of "finish," history has not yet come to an end. It goes on and shows all the characteristics of existential estrangement ... [But] In the sense of "aim," history has come to an intrinsic end qualitatively, namely, in the appearance of the New Being as a historical reality' (ST2, 138).

In this connection, it is striking that, in the *Systematic Theology*, Tillich does not interpret what he calls the 'symbol' of the Second Coming in terms of outstanding future possibilities regarding historical action. Instead, he interprets it, first, as a way of underlining and affirming that he, Jesus, is the Christ, and as excluding any 'superior manifestation' of the New Being (ST2, 188). Second, it corroborates the meaning of the resurrection and affirms that 'the might of the demonic is broken in principle' – even if there remains a 'not yet' such that this victory is not,

DOI: 10.1057/9781137454478.0007

for now, seen in all its glory (ST2, 189). The Second Coming, seemingly the most future-oriented of all Christian doctrines, serves first to point back to and confirm a revelation occurring in the past.

As I have said, it would be possible to explain this apparent change in terms of a shift or development in Tillich's thought as it responded to the changing social and political circumstances of the twentieth century. However, that would be both to soften the sharpness of the apparent contradiction and, at the same time, to fail to do justice to the internal tensions of Tillich's thought. For if the dominant element of the religious socialist writings is the expectation of a future transformation, this transformation also contained an element of the 'already' as well as the 'not yet'. Recall how, in the spirit of the humanist element in Marxist thought, Tillich argued that if the proletariat had really become completely degraded into a reified instrument in the service of capitalist production, then it would be incapable of the courageous action required by the socialist decision. The working-class challenge to bourgeois dominance is possible only where the working class is able to express the universal interest of humanity. Its revolt is a revolt on behalf of the humanity it feels coursing in its veins and it is this that empowers it to act. Or, in Tillich's vocabulary of the time, it must itself be gripped by the powers of origin if it is to have the power to overcome estrangement. The demonic can only be defeated by a greater power.

Going further back, we have seen how Schelling's system was worked out in terms of a sequence of dialectical polarities in such a way that even the extreme development of one pole never entirely loses its connection with the other. History may separate the actual manifestations of life in time from their divine origin, but not entirely. Identity is always in some measure present within difference. As in the distinction between the demonic and the Satanic, a principle that was pure negativity just couldn't exist and it can only exist when it is paradoxically joined together with the creative life-giving principle. In terms of Tillich's own reworking of the Schellingian model, even when the ontological structures of individualization and participation, freedom and destiny, and dynamics and form become transformed into 'structures of destruction' in incessant conflict with one another (individualization versus participation, freedom versus destiny, dynamics versus form), they still remain in some kind of relation each other. No matter how conflicted, they are all – in each of their manifestations – manifestations of the one identical

DOI: 10.1057/9781137454478.0007

principle of Being-Itself. As Tillich would say of those who experienced the post-war crisis of meaninglessness, 'The faith which makes the courage of despair possible is the acceptance of the power of being, even in the grip of non-being. Even in the despair about meaning being affirms itself through us. The act of accepting meaninglessness is in itself a meaningful act. It is an act of faith' (CB, 171). Only if there is already some relation to God, no matter how unconscious or how distorted, can there be the possibility of moving to conscious faith.

We shall explore some of these issues further when we explore Tillich's idea of correlation in greater detail and, in particular, the interplay of question and answer.[6] Here, the point is specifically regarding Tillich's claim that history and ontology can never entirely be separated. Disconnected from the power of being, history would sink back into a state of infinite and formless flux and it is therefore only when there is some relation to being, and therefore already some implicit formative power at work in historical life, that history becomes genuinely 'historical'. On this view, the manifestation of the power of being within history is not only impossible, it is even necessary for history itself.

If there is indeed a shift in Tillich's thought from the future orientation of religious socialism to the Christ-centred theology of the *Systematic Theology*, this, then, is a shift in emphasis and at no point can we speak of a complete break. But – and this is to return to the question with which we began this section – does this not nevertheless mean significantly weakening the seriousness and urgency of the demand for political action of the future orientation of the earlier period?

Tillich would doubtless acknowledge that there may be forms of Christian piety in which this happens – indeed, he is very conscious that his own religious socialism breaks with the political quietism of earlier Lutheran theologies in which the one thing needful was the believer's inner relation to Christ and which consequently taught non-involvement as the correct Christian attitude to political life. But that is to treat the manifestation of the eternal in time, in the Incarnation, as if it were some kind of fact isolated from the history in which it occurred. That Christ is able to constitute a centre of history does not absolve those who believe in Christ from a continuing relation to history or from the continuing demand to participate freely and responsibly in historical action.

I have spoken of a tension in Tillich's thought between the ontological principle of identity and the historical principle of difference, but Tillich himself is prepared to speak, following Kierkegaard, of the paradox of the Incarnation and says without hesitation that 'The Christian assertion that the New Being has appeared in Jesus as the Christ is paradoxical' (ST2, 104).

'Paradox' is, of course, a delicate term for a philosopher to start making use of and many of Kierkegaard's critics have been eager to condemn him for the irrationalism of his claims about Christ being the God-man, whilst defenders have sometimes suggested that the Kierkegaardian paradox is not really a paradox in the sense of being *against* reason but of being, simply, 'above' reason.[7] Tillich, for his part, rejects the identification of paradox with mere nonsense or absurdity. But he also insists that paradox is something more than dialectics. As we have several times seen, Tillich presents the relationship between the ontological polarities as inherently dialectical – each conditions the other in such a way that 'you can't have one without the other'. Freedom is only possible where there is destiny, and destiny can only be embraced by freedom. However, God as Being-Itself is as much beyond dialectics as he is beyond conventional logic. Early on in the *Systematic Theology*, Tillich emphasizes that divine revelation is revelation of the divine mystery in the specific sense of 'a dimension which "precedes" the subject-object relationship' (ST1, 121). Yet, as we have seen, the subject–object relationship is the only framework within which we can meaningfully speak of knowledge or cognition so that, consequently, 'revelation does not dissolve the mystery into knowledge' (ST1, 121).

But there would seem still to be a difference between mystery and paradox. Many people might concede that the power by virtue of which the world, life, and we ourselves have come into existence is a mystery that we will never fully comprehend. But that is not paradoxical. As Kierkegaard especially clearly emphasized, what is paradoxical is that the God who is eternal and as such eternally beyond time should appear in time, at a particular point in history, and that this particular moment of time should therefore become decisive for all time. In this sense, Christianity is inherently paradoxical in a way that neither Judaism nor Islam is. Pure monotheism may still be too mysterious for secular tastes, but it is not, in itself, paradoxical. We may or may not believe that God is God and the world is his creation, but it would seem fairly clear what believing or not believing in such a claim might involve. But the further claim that God is present in a unique and exclusive way in the life of this particular man is something else again. And it is this further claim that, Kierkegaard and, following him, Tillich, sees as paradoxical. And so, for

DOI: 10.1057/9781137454478.0007

both of them, the relation to Christ must be more than the acceptance of certain historical or metaphysical claims but, rather, become an existential relation of faith in which the whole of the believer's life is at stake. I can never *prove* or *know* that it is true; I can only commit myself to it by an act of faith – and I must do so totally.

Yet, to say it again, Tillich does not see the paradox as merely absurd although, as he puts it, it is 'against man's ordinary interpretation of his predicament with respect to himself, his world, and the ultimate underlying both of them' (ST2, 106). And what is this 'ordinary interpretation'? Perhaps we could imagine it as leading to either optimism or pessimism. Some might feel that the world is a good place in which human life is gradually getting better and better whilst others, scanning the news headlines or in the light of their own suffering, might conclude that the world 'lieth in evil' and that to expect any change for the better is empty idealism. On Tillich's view, the catastrophes of the twentieth century rendered the former option downright incredible. After two World Wars and the experience of genocidal totalitarianism, naive optimism was no longer an option. Despair, however, certainly was. Jean-Paul Sartre, expounding the existentialism that seemed to sum up the postwar outlook, stated that despair is the presupposition of contemporary thought. Deep down we all know that there is no point to it all – which doesn't mean that all we can do is to stare moodily into the depths of a glass of whisky, merely that we should be under no illusions as to the very narrow limitations of all human achievements. 'Progress' and 'good' are only ever relative to where we ourselves are situated here and now. Tillich's paradox, however, suggests that even if, and even when, all appearances might lead us to believe that 'the world lieth in evil' we still have access to the power that can overcome all evil. As he sums up, 'The appearance of the New Being under the conditions of existence, yet judging and conquering them, is the paradox of the Christian message' (ST2, 107).[8]

We have several times now used the expression 'the New Being', which is one of the key expressions of Tillich's theology. But it is also an expression that, in itself, somehow sums up and concentrates the paradox of salvation. This is because its two terms, 'new' and 'being', seem to focus, very precisely, the two elements of history and ontology that we have been considering in this chapter. The socialist decision, like any great historical decision, was aimed at a new ordering of historical relationships. Yet Tillich seems to have believed that this decision was only possible

DOI: 10.1057/9781137454478.0007

by virtue of the power of Being-Itself, even though, in the perspective of Being-Itself, the difference between past, present, and future is strictly relativized. How can 'Being-Itself' ever be or become 'new'? Simply as a name, albeit a rather philosophical name, for God, isn't it marked by the fact that a God who is truly God is and must be 'from everlasting' and therefore cannot be 'new'?

Of course, as we have just been seeing, Tillich is not going to underplay the paradox of this formulation and this paradox is part of the point. Where utopian visions would lead us to pursue novelty without reference to Being-Itself and where a mysticism of being that was detached from history would lead to passivity, real, concrete historical hope demands that both elements are actively present.

In a sermon entitled 'The New Being' Tillich sums up the Christian message as 'the message of a "new creation"' (NB, 15), a biblical expression that he immediately glosses as equivalent to 'the new being', adding that this is 'the new reality which has appeared with the appearance of Jesus who for this reason, and just for this reason, is called the Christ' (NB, 15). But the 'new creation' is not to be construed as something that will take place after the destruction of the present cosmic world order. It is an event that is to become a reality for us in real historical time. As Tillich quotes Paul, 'If any one is in union with Christ he is a new being; the old state of things has passed away; there is a new state of things.' In these terms, then, Christian existence is existence that already participates – somehow – in the new creation or new being. But how?

Tillich's answer is that 'The New Being is not something that simply takes the place of the Old Being. But it is a renewal of the Old which has been corrupted, distorted, split and almost destroyed. But not wholly destroyed. Salvation does not destroy creation; but it transforms the old creation into a new one' (NB, 20) – and it does so, he adds, through reconciliation, re-union, and resurrection. In other words, the New Being reverses the process by which the ontological elements are transformed into structures of destruction. Where individualization and participation, freedom and destiny, dynamics and form have become hostile, warring powers, the appearance of the New Being restores them to a relationship of creative interdependence. With particular regard to resurrection, Tillich by no means denies the reality of death, but he does deny that death is able to rob human life of eternal meaning. Resurrection in this sense is not a miraculous post-mortem event but 'the creation into eternity out of every moment in time ... Out of disintegration and death

DOI: 10.1057/9781137454478.0007

something is born of eternal significance. That which is immersed in dissolution emerges is a new creation'. And, he adds, 'Resurrection happens *now*, or it does not happen at all' (NB, 24).[9]

In the *Systematic Theology*, Tillich makes the same point in more formal terms, stating that 'The New Being is new ... in two respects: it is new in contrast to the merely potential character of essential being; and it is new over against the estranged character of existential being' (ST2, 137). Where, as we have seen, Tillich reinterprets the Genesis story of creation and fall to mean that existence as such means separation from essential being and, as it were, a 'fall' into duality, the new being signifies the possibility of re-affirming our relation to what is essential in human existence even in the state of estrangement. In terms of the traditional Lutheran doctrine of justification (the event in which a sinner returns into a right relation to God), the person who experiences the power of the new being is therefore 'at once just and sinful': they are at once 'just' since they have come back into relation to God, yet 'sinful' because they continue to be bound to situations in which sin remains a defining element (e.g. in the form of market forces or negative character traits). Paralleling the paradox of the revelation of the power of the new being in Jesus as the Christ, each individual experience of this power will, in a sense, be 'in spite of' everything in their lives that seems to contradict it – what Tillich calls 'the in-spite-of character' of Christian existence (ST2, 206). The paradox of the Incarnation is repeated in the paradox of the Christian life: Christians experience themselves as 'saved', yet also as called to strive for the furthering of God's Kingdom in the world, a paradox that theology has traditionally dealt with in terms of justification and sanctification: through justification the believer is put into a right relation to God whilst through sanctification the whole of his or her life is transformed – but if the former can be experienced as a once-off saving event, the latter is a process that continues through all of life.

The eternal now

The revelation of the new being in Jesus as the Christ means that Tillich is so far from limiting salvation to the future perspectives of religious socialism that he can speak of 'the eternal now', even taking this expression as the title of the last collection of sermons to be published in his life time.

DOI: 10.1057/9781137454478.0007

As I have been arguing, this need not be taken as meaning a break with his earlier thought, merely a change of emphasis and, in both pre- and post-war versions, the same fundamental tension – or, perhaps, paradox – is in play. God is – and is to come. The power of God has been revealed – but everything is still to fight for. In every present moment the Christian therefore lives as it were between the time of the fall and the time of final redemption, between a lost past and a future still to come. And now, at least, Tillich will say that it is in the present, the now, that the question of human beings' relation to time must find its solution. 'The riddle of the present is the deepest of all the riddles of time,' he says in the sermon 'The Eternal Now'. Yet it is also in experiencing all that there is to be experienced in the present – this vanishing moment between past and future – that we find the solution to the whole 'riddle' of time, namely, 'the eternal':

> Whenever we say 'now' or 'today' , we stop the flux of time for us. We accept the present and do not care that it is gone in the moment that we accept it. We live in it and it is renewed for us in every new 'present'. This is possible because every moment of time reaches into the eternal. It is the eternal that stops the flux of time for us. It is the eternal 'now' which provides for us a temporal 'now'. (EN, 110)

It is therefore telling that Tillich will insist on interpreting the 'divinity' of Christ in terms of the 'eternal' character of the Being revealed in him. 'God', says Tillich, has no essence separated from existence, 'he is beyond essence and existence. He is what he is, eternally by himself'.[10] But this is a problem for traditional theological reflection on the meaning of Christ since it tries to explain the relationship between the divine and human aspects of his existence in terms of his divine and human 'natures' or essences. But if existence is beyond essence, as Tillich says, then such theological formulations will necessarily fail to communicate the actual historical existence of Christ as the revelation in time or in existence of the divine power of being. Tillich therefore proceeds to call for the replacement of the idea of Christ's 'divine nature' 'by the concepts "eternal God-man-unity" or "Eternal God-Manhood"' (ST2, 170).[11] And, he comments, '"Eternal" points to the general presupposition of the unique event of Jesus as the Christ. This event could not have taken place if there had not been an eternal unity of God and man within the divine life' (ST2, 171).

This, as we saw in Chapter 1, was already the logic of Schelling's late philosophy, namely, that the possibility of reconciling the play of differences in historical time depended on a reconciliation that had always already taken place eternally in the life of God. But, again, this would once more seem to drag Tillich back towards a twofold retreat from the temporal openness of human existence since, on the one hand, the meaning of human life is made to depend on a past revelation (the revelation of Jesus as the Christ), whilst, on the other, this revelation is itself seen to be grounded in an eternal, that is, supra-temporal condition of divine–human unity that may equally well be manifest in past, present or future. The logical outcome of this position, however, seems to be that all ages are equally near to and equally far from the eternal God and that significant novelty is an illusion.

Tillich, however, resists this conclusion and continues to insist that the 'not yet' of eschatological expectation remains integral to Christian experience of the 'already' of the Incarnation. There is what Tillich calls an 'oscillation' between the 'already' (the Christ has come in time) and the 'not yet' (he will return to deliver a final judgement) that, he says, 'belongs inseparably to Christian existence' (ST2, 138). Christ is the end of history –yet the end is still to come. It is no coincidence, then, that, in the highly organized formal structure of Tillich's system the doctrine of Christ, 'the centre of history', constitutes the second, central volume of the system, whilst the third and final volume culminates and – literally – ends with the question of 'History and the Kingdom of God'.

In this third volume, Tillich suggests that we think of life as a dynamic process in which manifold dimensions are constantly being united and transformed. For human beings life is impossible without biological life or even the inorganic realm of chemical forces that precede and make possible the emergence of biological life. But it is also not fully 'life' unless or until it also becomes capable of expressing the truth and value of freedom and personality in culture and history. And, as the argument of volume three develops, we are shown that it is in history that all the other spheres are brought together, since history cannot occur other than as the field of action of human beings whose lives incorporate both inorganic and organic natural structures whilst opening out to allow the freedom, novelty, and uniqueness of truly human activity. Yet even history is not final, since even – especially – such truly creative activity must ultimately point beyond itself to the aim or *telos* of history that is in some sense also 'above' history. Just as expressionist art makes visible the question burning at the heart of existence, all cultural and historical creativity must culminate in revealing that we are, in the end, beings whose existence is from first to last questionable. We are not, and cannot be, the answer to our own question. We shall return in the final chapter to reflect further on the dialectic of question and answer and the way in which the question may already be directing us towards the answer, but we have by now read enough to see that although history, on Tillich's terms, 'cannot give an answer to the "New-Itself"' (ST2, 138), historical causality, 'Like historical time, ... is future-directed; it creates the new ... Historical causality drives towards the new beyond every particular new ... Therefore man's historical consciousness has always looked ahead beyond any particular new to the absolutely new, symbolically expressed as "New Creation"' (ST3, 347). And, as we saw in the previous section of this chapter, it is precisely this 'new creation' that Tillich sees as the best epitome of the Christian message to the modern world.

This 'new creation' is, of course, something very different from what is sought in technological or social progress, and we can scarcely imagine Tillich having much time for contemporary scientific utopias that involve the engineering of human beings into transhuman entities.[12] The new being has already appeared decisively in Jesus as the Christ and the revelation of his 'eternal God-Manhood'. It is new in the sense of the hymn 'New every morning is the love', that is, it is *the same* love that is experienced each day anew and as new.

This seems to mean that the end (*telos*) of history is 'the elevation of the temporal into eternity' (ST3, 422ff.). It is not just that (as we have seen) the eternal is present in the depth of every 'now' but also that 'the ever present end of history elevates the positive content of history into eternity at the same time that it excludes the negative from it' (ST3, 423–4), a point that seems to Tillich to be the essential meaning of such symbols as 'eternal life' and the 'last judgement' (which, because it is envisaged in these terms as an occurrence that takes place in the depth of temporal life itself rather than after death, he prefers to call 'ultimate judgement'). To explain more exactly what this means, he also proposes the idea of an 'eternal memory'. 'Time' he writes

> is the form of the created finite ... and eternity is the inner aim, the telos of the created finite, permanently elevating the finite into itself. With a bold metaphor one could say that the temporal, in a continuous process, becomes 'eternal memory.' But eternal memory is living retention of the remembered thing. It is together past, present, and future in a transcendent unity of the three modes of time. More cannot be said – except in poetic imagery. (ST3, 426)

DOI: 10.1057/9781137454478.0007

In so far as this is also the 'ultimate judgement' of historical life, it has a negative aspect that, for Tillich, means that whatever fails to contribute towards the approach of the Kingdom of God, 'is not remembered at all. It is acknowledged for what it is, non-being' – although, again, this can only be further glossed in poetic language (ST3, 426).

Yet Tillich himself does seem to say more, when he says that eternal life, *qua life* and as one with the Kingdom of God, involves 'the non-fragmentary, total, and complete conquest of the ambiguities of life – and this under all dimensions of life, or, to use another metaphor, in all degrees of being' (ST3, 428). This means that, it is life characterized inter alia by centredness, freedom, and creativity and the 'blessedness' that 'is not a state of immovable perfection ... But ... blessedness through fight and victory' (ST3, 431). This is, in some respects, remarkably similar to the long-established, indeed normative, theological definition of eternity as 'the complete, simultaneous and perfect possession of everlasting life'.[13] Although Boethius (who first formulated this definition) contrasts eternity with life in time, the fact that he insists on it as *life* seems also to some commentators to suggest something different from a purely abstract state of timelessness. For Tillich, however, eternal life – that is, the full content of eternal memory – incorporates all that is truly meaningful in historical existence, especially and above all everything that is done towards bringing about the advent of the Kingdom.

Tillich also sees this as solving one of the actual problems of communist society. For the pursuit of any utopia is consciously the pursuit of something of still to be realized in some nearer or more distant future. Although we may one day succeed in building Jerusalem in 'England's green and pleasant land' (Blake), many individuals and perhaps even many generations are likely to perish before this happens. But the symbol of eternal life points to the possibility of fulfilment for individuals who cannot realistically expect to see the arrival of God's Kingdom on earth. For eternal life is life 'in' God: 'in ultimate fulfilment God shall be everything in (or for) everything', a view Tillich calls 'eschatological pan-en-theism' (ST3, 450). In these terms, eternal life is a dimension of everything that is occurring now, in the present. The phrase 'in God', he says, 'points to the presence of everything that has being in the divine ground of being ... [and] to the inability of anything finite to be without the supporting power of permanent divine creativity – even in the state of estrangement and despair ... [it is] the state of essentialization of all creatures' (ST3, 450).

DOI: 10.1057/9781137454478.0007

In this chapter we have explored different facets of a tension or even a paradox at the heart of Tillich's thought, namely, the tension between a God who, as Being-Itself, can be revealed and known in every present moment, including in situations of extreme alienation. As in Tillich's own experience of the Botticelli painting in the Berlin gallery, art can offer a preliminary case of such revelation but art's own most powerful works point beyond themselves to a further and more fundamental revelation: the revelation of the new being in the life of Jesus as the Christ. Yet, as Tillich himself asserts, such a revelation becomes paradoxical in the light of human beings' historically conditioned expectations about what they are and what they are capable of. Where history seems to offer only relative fulfilments that are always exposed to ambiguity and distortion, the Christian revelation seems to offer absolute or unconditional or ultimate meaning. But how then can we, as historically and temporally existing beings, ever really receive revelation of this kind? To the extent that revelation enters into the woof and warp of life in time, its character of ultimacy seems to become imperilled, but if or when it does succeed in showing us something of eternal life, it seems to weaken the seriousness with which we have to take the challenges of existence, encouraging passivity and withdrawal. And, as we have now several times seen, it would seem to be just this insistence on the presence of the eternal in time and the revelation of Being-Itself in the power of the new being that both indicates the continuing power of Schelling's system over his thought and separates him from the efforts of several generations of philosophers, such as Lévinas, who have sought to free religious thought from ontology and to give time and difference precedence over identity. Another way of putting this is simply to say that perhaps we must then conclude that Tillich is to be numbered amongst the philosophers (and, in particular, amongst the metaphysical philosophers) rather than the theologians. Instead of seeing him as a philosophical theologian, maybe we would do better off to see him as a theological philosopher, whose work ultimately aims at the completeness of his system rather than the openness of faith.[14]

Perhaps if Tillich's system were limited to resolving questions of being and time or revelation and history, such conclusions might be in place. But there is a further dimension to his thought that we have as yet merely touched on, namely, the place and role of love. And it is in relation to the question of love, I suggest, that we start to see how Tillich's philosophical work does, in the end, serve a theological purpose.

DOI: 10.1057/9781137454478.0007

Notes

1   It is perhaps worth noting that Schelling too had at one point given particular emphasis to the role of *aesthetic* intuition, although, as we shall see, Tillich's idea of what was involved in the experience of art was very different from Schelling's own.

2   At least, that is how Protestants have traditionally seen it. For a strong contrary view, see E. Duffy, *The Stripping of the Altars: Traditional Religion in England, 1400–1580* (Newhaven, CT: Yale University Press, 1992).

3   For further discussion of the relationship between sacrament and word in Tillich's thought, see Chapter 5.

4   For an alternative Marxist view that is quite close to Tillich's, see Herbert Marcuse, *The Aesthetic Dimension* (Basingstoke: Palgrave Macmillan, 1979).

5   Karl Barth, *The Epistle to the Romans* (Oxford: Oxford University Press, 1933), pp. 483–4.

6   See Chapter 5.

7   Kierkegaard himself gives some support to this view. See the chapter 'The Absolute Paradox' in S. Kierkegaard, trans. H. V. and E. H. Hong, *Philosophical Fragments/ Johannes Climacus* (Princeton: Princeton University Press, 1985), pp. 37–48.

8   In a critical study largely drawing on Kierkegaard, Kenneth Hamilton argued that Tillich's understanding of paradox in fact subordinates it to the demands of his philosophical system. In different terminology that partially reflects the focus of the present study on the tension between identity and difference. See Kenneth Hamilton, *The System and the Gospel: A Critique of Paul Tillich* (London: SCM Press, 1963). The thrust of the present discussion implicitly recognizes the force of Hamilton's objections, though it does not, in the end, accede to them.

9   These claims are clearly controversial with regard to traditional Christianity. However, they are not without precedent. Many commentators have noticed that there is a tendency towards such a 'realized eschatology' in the Gospel of John, for example, and Tillich's argument might be seen as taking that tendency to its logical conclusion.

10   By 'by himself' I take Tillich to mean 'by means of himself' rather than 'on his own'.

11   It is tempting to see this as an expression derived from Russian religious philosophy. Although Tillich does not refer to this as a source, he did meet with Berdyaev shortly before the Second World War and expressed some sympathy with Berdyaev's position, in which the idea of God-Manhood played a key role.

12   For Tillich's writings on technology see P. Tillich, ed. M. J. Thomas, *The Spiritual Situation in our Technical Society* (Macon, GA: Mercer University

DOI: 10.1057/9781137454478.0007

Press, 1988). For discussion see my *Thinking about God in an Age of Technology* (Oxford: Oxford University Press, 2007), pp. 44–7.

13   Boethius, *The Consolation of Philosophy*, trans. V. E. Watts (Harmondsworth: Penguin, 1969), pp. 163–4.

14   See Hamilton, *The System and the Gospel* for this line of criticism.

DOI: 10.1057/9781137454478.0007

4
Love

Abstract: *Tillich's theology identifies God as Being-Itself, which leads to the question as to whether Christian theology prioritizes Being over love or vice versa. But if love is prior to Being then it seems that Tillich ultimately subordinates love to ontology. Tillich's account of love is interdependent with his critique of autonomy and his call for theonomy. This preserves the individuality of the person without absolutizing it. Faced with situations of separation love means that mutual acceptance, forgiveness, and reconciliation are always possible. Rooted in Christian teaching on forgiveness, Tillich's position also allows for application in pastoral care and counselling.*

Pattison, George. *Paul Tillich's Philosophical Theology: A Fifty-Year Reappraisal.* Basingstoke: Palgrave Macmillan, 2015. DOI: 10.1057/9781137454478.0008.

DOI: 10.1057/9781137454478.0008

In relation to the Fall, to history, and to the ever-present possibility of the demonic, Tillich's system repeatedly skirts the outer limits of what can be thought systematically, that is, what can be thought in accordance with a fundamental principle of identity that guarantees in advance that unity will prevail over difference and being over non-being. Of course, Tillich never forgot that young lives could be horrifically cut off as hundreds of thousands were cut off in the Battle of Verdun or that demonic powers such as those that became manifest in Nazism could wreak terrible havoc on earth. Yet, as we have seen, he nevertheless insisted that this did not compel us to lose faith in the eternal triumph of the good and of the power of being over non-being. In eternity, if not in time, all good things remain possible.

I suggest that this does not mean that Tillich's system mechanically turns out a good result, no matter what data we feed into it. His is not the metaphysical optimism of a Hegel and if, in eternity, evil has always already been conquered, in time it can only be challenged through a free and courageous response to moments of destiny and decision. Everything is still to play for. But that also means that the human response is itself integral to the triumph of the Eternal in time. There is no 'cunning of reason' working behind our backs to secure the good result irrespective of what we think or do or say. And this in turn means that human values, actions, and commitments are part of what is to be taken up into the 'eternal memory' of which Tillich speaks in the last volume of his *Systematic Theology*. Chief amongst these are the values, actions, and commitments that are manifest in such interconnected terms as freedom, personality, and love. And if it is in love that what is at issue is most intensely focused, then the question as to the limits of the system is also a question as to the relationship between being and love. This, then, becomes a crucial and even decisive point in the overall meaning of Tillich's system. Is love, in the end, a mere form of the manifestation of Being-Itself – or is love, perhaps, the beginning of an order that transcends being and, in doing so, transcends the whole sphere of dialectical ontological relationships of freedom and destiny, individualization and participation, dynamics and form?

In posing the question in these terms, it is not only a matter of interpreting Tillich but, in a sense, the whole tradition of Christian theology in the West, since it is just these two terms, being and love, that have provided the two points of the ellipse that has determined the concept of God in Western thinking. As I noted in Chapter 1, Christian tradition

DOI: 10.1057/9781137454478.0008

has repeatedly insisted that, as Thomas Aquinas put it, 'He Who Is' is the most fitting of the names by which human beings can name their God. In making this claim Thomas, like Augustine before him, pointed back to the story of Moses at the burning bush where God is said to have named himself 'I AM THAT I AM'. Yet Christian tradition also states that God is Love. Perhaps these terms are not mutually exclusive, but it seems natural to ask which comes first: love – or being? Agape or Esse? And this is not only a question about God: it is also a question about human beings – unavoidably so, if, as Jewish and Christian teaching has it, we are made in the image and likeness of God. So what about us? Is our primary task to discover the meaning of being and to enact the 'courage to be'? Or is it to give ourselves to works of love? To repeat: which comes first: love – or being? Agape or Esse? At the end of his great poem, Dante speaks of God as 'the love that moves the sun and other stars', but does this mean that love is the power behind the great cosmic forces on which all life depends and that being is therefore dependent on love or does it mean that 'love' is a state of being in harmony with the universe and that love is therefore dependent on being?

Commonsense tells us that the answer to the question 'love or being' must be being, for unless something *is* (or, rather, since love implies plurality, that some things are), there is nothing and no one to love or be loved. But do we know what it is for something to be? As Heidegger asked at the beginning of *Being and Time*, 'Do we today have an answer to that which is really meant by the word "being" [*seiend*]?' To which he immediately replied 'Not at all.'[1] Commonsense might think that the question about the being can be answered in the manner of a simple realism: that being is simply a way of indicating that the things we see and touch and hear and so on really are out there, bodies moving about in time and space. At this level, commonsense is, of course, right to say that entities of some kind must exist in some way in order for there to be love. But what kind of entities must exist and in what way must they exist in order for there to be love? Common sense doesn't tell us that, or not in such a way as to compel unanimity.

The self-evidence of the answer that being must come first is problematized as soon as we reformulate the question with specific regard to human beings. Arguably, what we know of love as human beings may also be found amongst non-human animals. Again, common sense would probably see love simply as an evolved capacity serving the survival and propagation of the human animal and, as such, essentially rooted in our

DOI: 10.1057/9781137454478.0008

animal nature. However, if we take seriously the testimony of Christian literature that love is something that must be commanded as well as instinctively enacted, or, for that matter, the testimony of secular art and literature that we can fail in love, lose our way in love, and return to love as well as being (frequently) bedazzled and deceived by love as well as (sometimes) sacrificing ourselves for love, then the straightforwardness of the common-sense evolutionary explanation of love starts to crumble. Love can only be love where there is freedom and personality and that means where human beings are not constrained or pre-determined by what they are but – somehow – step beyond the sway of 'what is' into a new kind of life in which, as the gospels put it, 'all things are possible'.

But what of Tillich? Is his system in the end a system in which love, no matter how central, is finally subordinate to being, or does being, in fact, ultimately serve to bring us to the threshold at which love, as it were, takes over?

As we might expect, Tillich's approach is nothing if not dialectical and several of his comments could be read either way. In *Love, Power and Justice* he says that these three terms 'point to a trinity of structures in being itself. Love, power, and justice are metaphysically speaking as old as being itself. They precede everything that is, and they cannot be derived from anything that is. They have ontological dignity.' And, in support of this, he notes that, for the ancient Greeks, 'They were gods before they became rational qualities of being' (LPJ, 21). Nevertheless, if, 'God is Being-Itself' is the sole non-symbolic statement that we can make about God, then, as Tillich himself says, it would seem that 'one speaks symbolically of God as love' (STI, 310), which would seem to make 'love' a symbolic form of being and therefore give final priority to being.[2]

This would seem to be confirmed by the way in which Tillich's fundamental definitions of love relate to the dialectic of separation and union. In *Love, Power, and Justice* he writes 'Love is the drive towards the union of the separated. Reunion presupposes separation of that which essentially belongs together. It would, however, be wrong to give to separation the same ontological ultimacy as reunion. For separation presupposes an original unity. Unity embraces itself and separation, just as being comprises itself and non-being' (LPJ, 25). Here, then, it would seem that love is essentially a movement or 'moment' within the overall dialectical pattern of ontological separation and union, the reintegration of the structures of destruction into the structures of being.

But are matters that simple?

DOI: 10.1057/9781137454478.0008

Tillich himself immediately goes on to acknowledge that 'Love manifests its greatest power there where it overcomes the greatest separation.' And, he adds, 'the greatest separation is the separation of self from self' (LPJ, 21). The question then becomes just how 'separate' such separation can actually be. If the humanity of each individual human being is no more than the manifestation of a single essential 'humanity', then it would seem that separation can only be relative. In loving you for your humanity I love something that I already implicitly know in myself. Indeed, several philosophers have seen the meaning and purpose of love in just such a process of building up our common humanity through loving the humanity in the other.[3] What binds us together is what we have in common. But this would seem not quite to do justice to what many experience as the singularity of each individual human person. In loving *you* I don't just love the humanity in you, I love *you* – and I don't and never will love anyone else in quite the same way![4] Tillich himself seems to move in this direction when he says that 'The separation of a completely individualized being from any other completely individualized being is itself complete. The centre of a completely individualized being cannot be entered by any other individualized being, and it cannot be made into a mere part of a higher unity' (LPJ, 26). Yet, as Tillich also reminds us, 'the individual longs to return to the unity to which he belongs, in which he participates by his ontological nature. This longing for reunion is an element in every love, and its realisation, however fragmentary, is experienced as bliss' (ST1, 310).

We seem to balance on a knife-edge. Love must involve the free commitment and consent of the one who is lover or beloved but the possibility of love exists only by virtue of an ontological structure that precedes any individual or shared act of freedom. Perhaps this is what Kant called a fundamental antinomy, a dilemma that simply cannot be decisively resolved in one direction or the other. But even if that is so, then we might still look to deepen our understanding of what is at stake in it, and to do so we might usefully look at what else Tillich says about the human person, about the unity and freedom of the person, and the nature of truly personal relations to others. In fact, to conclude that we had reached the point of an irresolvable antinomy would also be to suggest that there is a sense in which, in the end, his system is more than a system of identity. 'Love' would not then signify the point at which the system is transcended, but it would mark the limit of the system with regard to the actual challenges of life as it is to be lived.

DOI: 10.1057/9781137454478.0008

Life, freedom, spirit

Tillich several times connects love to life. That God – Being-Itself – is love is understandable, he says, 'only because the actuality of being is life' (ST I, 310). Being-Itself, as we have seen, does not 'exist', since nothing exists except when, as Tillich puts it, it stands out of non-being and, in this way, also incorporates the dialectic of being and non-being into its existence. Nothing that is simply 'is' but is always in the process of coming into or passing out of being. Tillich speaks of 'life' as the actualization of potential being, but it might be more accurate in his own terms to say that every manifestation of life involves a particular combination of potentiality and actualization. As the living person that I am, I have actualized or fulfilled some of my potentialities whilst others have been definitively renounced and others remain to be discovered and fulfilled. Indeed, the fact that I actualize one particular potentiality may lead to the generation of new potentialities that would not otherwise have been developed. By committing to the study of theology and then working on Paul Tillich for my BD dissertation I became reasonably proficient in reading German, which probably wouldn't have happened if I'd pursued other life-possibilities such as becoming a forestry worker or psychiatric nurse (although in those cases too, yet other possibilities would have been generated leading down unknown paths not to be taken).

In the dynamic ferment of life every living thing strives to be itself, and that is as true when we are talking about an amoeba or a mayfly as when we are talking about a dinosaur or a human being. This is what Tillich calls the drive to self-integration and that in turn involves individualization and the 'centredness' that belongs to being an individual – even when, in the case of the amoeba, this may be an individual centredness that is also identical with that of all other members of the species. But, as we have seen, individualization is itself one element in a dialectical polarity of which participation is the other, opposite element. Without participation an entity becomes absolutely isolated and an absolutely individualized, relation-less entity would be an entity effectively devoid of life – perhaps like the figure of Satan in Dante's *Inferno*, frozen into complete immobility. This would be one form of what Tillich calls disintegration, while its opposite would be the dissolution of centredness in the flux of the entity's relationship with its ever-changing world.[5]

This structure is evident, Tillich thinks, at all levels of life, but in human life a further factor comes into play that significantly transforms

DOI: 10.1057/9781137454478.0008

the situation. This is human freedom, which, in the first instance, is manifested in, and as, morality. 'Morality is the constitutive function of spirit,' Tillich writes, defining a moral act as 'an act in which life integrates itself in the dimension of spirit, and this means as personality within a community. Morality is the function of life in which the centred self constitutes itself as a person' (ST3, 40). We shall shortly return to the question of 'spirit' but it is important to emphasize that when Tillich says 'morality' he is not thinking of obedience to a set of moral rules. For Tillich, closely following Kant in this respect, the essence of moral life is freedom: to live a moral life is to live in accordance with freedom and has relatively little to do with what we might call 'moralism' or being 'moralistic'.[6] To be moral is to be able to confront a given reality with the demand that it ought to become other than it is – we might think back to Tillich's idea of the socialist decision as involving the demand to bring about what-ought-to-be, namely, a society freed from the class divisions engendered by the bourgeois social order. Ultimately, however, what-ought-to-be is, simply, the rule of love or *agape*.[7] 'The principle of agape expresses the unconditional validity of the moral imperative, and it gives the ultimate norm for all ethical action' (ST3, 51). In these terms, morality demonstrates its essential character of freedom in the fact that those who love can become capable of supreme self-sacrifice, surrendering even life itself for the sake of the love that is seen as the goal of life.

But if moral freedom is in this way constitutive of spirit, spirit is also more than simple freedom. Along with 'Life', 'Spirit' is one of the defining axes of the penultimate part of the *Systematic Theology* and it is a term that Tillich adopts in full consciousness of its philosophically and theologically controversial history. For much of the nineteenth century, broadly following Hegel, 'spirit' was a term regularly used in a quasi-theological sense to describe, for example, the triumphs of the human spirit or the spiritual mission of the West. Following the First World War, however, a new wave of theologians, led by Karl Barth, saw this as indicative of the disastrous confusion of the divine and the human in nineteenth-century liberal thought. To speak of the defining power of human life as 'spirit' was already to imply that there was something at least semi-divine about humanity and, simultaneously, to forget the distinctive and independent power of the truly divine Holy Spirit, a Spirit able to break into human life and transform it through a more-than-human power. Yet, distinguishing between 'spirit' with a small 's' and divine Spirit with a capital 'S', Tillich goes against many of his contemporaries' assumption that these must be

DOI: 10.1057/9781137454478.0008

kept firmly apart. Where the demonic works the destruction of a human being's free personal being or spirit, divine Spirit does not so much 'seize' a human being as elevate it above itself. As Tillich puts it 'The spirit, a dimension of finite life, is driven into a successful self-transcendence; it is grasped by something ultimate and unconditional. It is still the human spirit ... but, at the same time, it goes out of itself under the impact of the divine Spirit' (ST3, 119). Life in the Spirit, in this sense, has what Tillich calls an ecstatic character, something we have already seen in those revelations, artistic or religious, that disclose a depth and a power in life that we had not hitherto been aware of. New possibilities are projected in ecstatic life that goes beyond every expectation we might develop solely on the basis of an analysis of 'what is', that is, what is currently known to be the case. And it is only when we are thus ecstatically opened up to what is beyond ourselves that we enter the domain of what is truly religious, such as the domain of the New Being and the reconciliation that it brings about.

In these terms, the relationship between human spirit and divine Spirit is a relationship in which there is never a simple identity, but a movement of ecstatic difference. Religious believers have often talked about the Holy Spirit as coming to dwell 'in' the believer, but, as Tillich points out, this spatial imagery is intrinsically misleading: 'If the divine Spirit breaks into the human spirit, this does not mean that it rests there, but that it drives the human spirit out of itself. The "in" of the divine Spirit is an "out" for the human spirit' (ST3, 119). In this respect, what Tillich calls the 'spiritual presence' not only exemplifies but also takes to a new level the fundamentally ecstatic character of existence as such, which, as we have seen, he construed as meaning 'standing out' of non-being.

It could be relevant at this point to say more about the demonic and there is no doubt that the realm of the ecstatic is one in which the potential for a demonic rather than a divine revelation is more than usually powerful. Carried beyond itself in ecstasy, the centred self is exposed to the risk of radically losing itself – but this risk is intrinsic to spiritual life. As Tillich remarks concerning self-sacrifice, we can never know in advance whether the sacrifice of present reality (e.g. the security of a good job) for the sake of an untried possibility (a new relationship or career) or, for that matter, the sacrifice of untried possibilities (the career I might have had) for the sake of something real and tangible (the job offer on the table right now) will be for the good – for our own good or for that of others. Occasions for getting it wrong abound. But, as he says in a related

DOI: 10.1057/9781137454478.0008

passage, creativity cannot be separated from the possibility of chaos (ST3, 54), a point that is already indicated in the Genesis creation story.

We shall return to the question of the demonic later, but before we do so there are several further points to take into consideration. The first concerns the dialectic of autonomy and heteronomy and its resolution in what Tillich calls theonomy. This will lead to a discussion of Tillich's restatement of the Christian doctrine of forgiveness in terms of what he calls the courage to accept acceptance. This will not only provide occasion for further comment on the demonic, but also help us to a more precise view as to how love might qualify the principle of identity that seems to underwrite Tillich's system.

Autonomy, heteronomy, theonomy

In its human form, the universal drive towards centred individualization takes the form of a free creative act. All life individualizes itself, and even one amoeba is, after all, a different amoeba from its neighbour. Ludwig Feuerbach identified human being with what he called our species-being, so that to love another person is to love their humanity rather than their individuality. On Tillich's view, however, the individual is more than an exemplar of the species *homo sapiens*. As we have been seeing, the individual is a centre of moral and spiritual freedom and in these terms the drive towards individualization involves us in taking responsibility for our relation to the world as a whole, to other people, and to ourselves. This is the principle of autonomy.

Tillich sees the principle of autonomy[8] as part of modernity's defining inheritance from the Enlightenment which, in turn, he sees as stemming from the Protestant Reformation's insistence on the need for individual faith (as opposed to acceptance of the Church hierarchy). He broadly accepts Kant's definition of autonomy as 'man's conquering the state of immaturity so far as he is responsible for it. Immaturity...is the inability to use one's own reason without the guidance of somebody else. Immaturity of this kind is caused by ourselves. It is rooted in the lack of resoluteness and courage to use reason without the guidance of another person' (PNTT, 24) – leading to Kant's call (which Tillich several times affirms) *sapere aude*: dare to know! 'Autonomy,' Tillich goes on to say, 'is man's living by the law of reason in all realms of his spiritual activity' (PNTT, 25).

DOI: 10.1057/9781137454478.0008

Against the principle of autonomy stands the opposing principle of heteronomy,[9] in which the individual is subordinated to the will of another. An archetypal instance of heteronomy would be the outlook of Dostoevsky's Grand Inquisitor, who depicts himself as compassionately bearing the responsibility that the simple and weak-minded multitude are unable to bear for themselves. Indeed, religion is likely to prove a fertile ground for heteronomy. We might think of the Catholic Church's suppression of Galileo or, in the nineteenth and early twentieth centuries, its opposition to all forms of modernism (including democracy, the theory of evolution, and critical historical enquiry), but Protestant fundamentalism and, for that matter, Dostoevsky's own beloved Russian Orthodoxy have often attempted to limit the rights of individuals to form their own beliefs and to act upon them.[10] Obedience is a salient virtue amongst many religious confessions, but whilst obedience to one's own conscience might be seen as an instance of autonomy, any other form of obedience is likely to be more or less heteronomous.

Even in the midst of the German Church struggle against Nazism, Tillich sees the danger of heteronomy emerging amongst the followers of Karl Barth, who, like him rejected the so-called German Christians' attempt to subordinate the Church to the National Socialist State. He comments, that 'The extremely narrow position of the Barthians may save German Protestantism, but it also creates a new heteronomy, an anti-autonomous and anti-humanistic attitude that I must regard as a denial of the Protestant principle' (IH, 26). Barth for his part regarded Tillich's theology as an overly obsessive struggle against the Grand Inquisitor.

As these comments indicate, Tillich generally approved the principle of autonomy in its rejection of heteronomy. It was, he believed, intrinsic to the drive towards an individualized spiritual freedom. However, it should be said that the issue is not simply one of individual versus society. The struggle between autonomy and heteronomy has taken many other forms in the emergence of the modern world, including national struggles for self-determination, science's collective attempts to free human thinking from the authority of the Church, the desire of artists to create an art for art's sake, and the pursuit of total deregulation by free market economists.

These last examples alert us to why there were limits to Tillich's endorsement of the principle of autonomy. We have seen how he regarded both nationalism and a deregulated free market as two of the major demonries of his time and both these cases show that whilst

DOI: 10.1057/9781137454478.0008

national liberation may be justified in relation to an occupying imperial power or marketization be justified in relation to feudal, guild, or statist control, they are in and of themselves insufficient to guarantee good outcomes. The problem as Tillich sees it is that although autonomy is to be affirmed against heteronomy, it is not of itself able to generate any positive content. Autonomy concerns the form or the appropriation of truth, not its substance. Left to itself the principle of autonomy drains the meaning out of the substantial powers of life, leaving us empty and uprooted. By way of contrast, heteronomous systems (e.g. religious traditionalism or political romanticism) have content, and this can make them attractive to an age that has experienced a kind of secularization that seems to leave the world devoid of values or substance – what Weber called 'the disenchantment of the world'. In this regard, perhaps the ultimate achievement of the principle of autonomy would be the creation of a world in which all aspects of life were subject to rational planning. But who would want to live in such a world? In an essay entitled 'The Technical City as Symbol' (perhaps not coincidentally published a year after the release of the movie *Metropolis*), Tillich writes that 'The soil, the bond with the living earth is taken away. Hewn or artificial stone separates us from it. Reinforced concrete buildings separate us more than loam, wood, and bricks from the cosmic flow. Water is in pipes; fire is confined to wires.'[11]

This kind of comment should not mislead us. We have seen that (unlike Heidegger) Tillich was never one to argue for the superiority of rural life over the life of the city and his commitment to socialism was also a commitment to using science and all the resources of modern society to create a more fitting context for the human values embodied in the lives of the industrial workers. Here too it is a case not only of affirming autonomy in the face of heteronomy but also of being clear about the limitations of autonomy itself. It is what his Frankfurt colleagues, Horkheimer and Adorno, would call the dialectic of Enlightenment in which the humanly created means of liberation from the atavistic powers of the old order can themselves become the form of new forms of alienation and enslavement.

Not the least important of these new forms of alienation is the loss of any sense of meaning or purpose, and Tillich sees his contemporary secular existentialism as evidence of just this. This is how he characterizes Heidegger's account of what is involved in the authentically resolute confrontation with death:

DOI: 10.1057/9781137454478.0008

Nobody can give directions for the actions of the 'resolute' individual –
no God, no conventions, no laws of reason, no norms or principles. We
must be ourselves, we must decide where to go. Our conscience is the call
to ourselves … it is neither the voice of God nor the awareness of eternal
principles … There is no norm, no criterion for what is right and wrong.
Resoluteness makes right what is right. (CB, 146)

Sartre offers an even more extreme case. According to Sartre's principle
that existence precedes essence and his assertion that we are the sum
of our actions 'Man creates what he is. Nothing is given to him to
determine his creativity. The essence of his being – the "should-be", the
"ought-to-be" – is not something which he finds; he makes it' (CB, 147).
But, as Sartre himself has concluded, the human subject is consequently
'a useless passion' and there is no real or substantial difference between
any of the choices we might make in relation to our life other than our
preparedness to take responsibility for them.

For Tillich, however, there was a third alternative, which he called theonomy, the law or rule of God. This, however, is not simply a reinstatement of heteronomy. It is not a call to modern men and women to return
to the Church or to submit themselves to biblical teaching. Theonomy
is the rule, precisely, of God, not of Church or Bible and, as such, it
can only come about as a spiritual event and therefore as an event in
which human freedom and creativity – human 'spirit' – is accepted and
affirmed. With specific regard to theonomy, Tillich says, we have 'our
own personal experience of the presence of the divine Spirit within us,
witnessing to the Bible or to the church … Where this inner witness is
lacking … obedience to authority would be mere external subjection
and not inward personal experience' (PNTT, 26). And theonomy too,
like both autonomy and heteronomy, could take a social form, as in the
symbol of the utopian future that the religious socialist strives to bring
about.

To prevent theonomy from developing into a new heteronomy a significant re-appraisal of what is already involved in autonomy is called
for. Just as the demand to act for the coming of socialism is impotent
without the recognition of the actual, living power of the working class
that is to bring about the revolution, any case of theonomy implies an
element of 'always already', even in the state of alienated autonomy or
repressive heteronomy. In a study of nineteenth- and twentieth-century
theology, Tillich describes autonomy 'as the memory which man has
of his own created goodness' (PNTT, 25). Alienation or estrangement

DOI: 10.1057/9781137454478.0008

is never absolute and an element of unity always remains. Even in the extreme situation of existential meaninglessness – and even without the individual being necessarily aware of it – the courage resolutely to accept anxiety reveals a residual link to the self-affirmation of being-itself, that is, to the power of God implicit in the fact of existence. Sartre at least believes in freedom but freedom, in a Tillichian perspective, is precisely indicative of human beings' spiritual – and eternal! – essence.

All of this means that absolute autonomy is impossible. Even in our most intense striving for autonomous individualization, we remain connected to others in a manifold of ways. Even as we separate ourselves out from the life of the family or the crowd we simultaneously experience the desire for reunion – what poets and philosophers have long identified as the 'eros' element in love. And it is important that the aspect of love is emphasized at this point since if theonomy is not to be a simple regression to heteronomy then it must preserve the moments of freedom and spiritual life. It is not a matter of returning to the bosom of the tribe or being reabsorbed into the crowd but of entering into renewed relationships with others as a fully free individual who is capable of and also willing to recognize the freedom and spiritual integrity of others.

But this cannot be some kind of automatic rebound, as if having gone to one extreme we mechanically switch to the other (and perhaps, eventually, find a point of balance in the middle). And if one aspect of the theonomic return to being-in-relationship involves recognizing others' spiritual freedom, the presupposition of any such return is that the aim (if not the achievement) of striving for maximum autonomy has in fact been disruptive of such relationship and recognition. I have been too busy pursuing my own rights to pay attention to yours or too busy being myself even to listen to you. A first obstacle to theonomy, then, is the obstacle that the autonomous individual has created through the act of separating out from the initial condition of unity. As Tillich cited Kierkegaard at the start of his Schelling dissertation, repentance is the normal relation of human beings to God. And, again in the terms of that dissertation, we may put the question we have now arrived at as, quite precisely, a question of mysticism and guilt-consciousness, that is, the question as to how unity – or, more exactly, reunification – is possible when we have become separated out from others through our own guilty action.

DOI: 10.1057/9781137454478.0008

Acceptance

Amongst Tillich's most enduring contributions is the rewriting of the Christian doctrine of justification and the event of forgiveness. Although this is a central theme in all Christian teaching, it became especially prominent in the teaching of Martin Luther, reflecting his own struggles with feelings of overwhelming guilt, his inability to achieve perfection, and his search for a gracious God who could forgive him as the sinner that he was. Tillich reflects this classical Lutheran preoccupation, writing that 'nothing greater can happen to a human being than that he is forgiven' (NB, 7). However, he also radically reinterprets the language of guilt, sin, wrath, and justification in which the traditional doctrine had been formulated and speaks instead in terms of acceptance or, more particularly, self-acceptance – or, more particularly still, self-acceptance 'in spite of' being unacceptable. Such acceptance, he suggests, is possible only because of the power of the New Being revealed in Jesus as the Christ, but it is also implicitly present in all of the modes of spiritual presence in which the power of theonomy is manifest.

In 1933 Tillich regarded the rise of Nazism as manifesting the demonic potential of human history. As we know, his worst fears were realized and Germany succumbed to the seduction of the Führer. The self-assertion of the German people (to use the language of the time) proved a catastrophic version of demonic autonomy. Returning to Germany after the war, Tillich observed the price that had been paid in the horrors experienced not only by the victims of Nazism but also by those who had more or less willingly, more or less consciously, been its agents. What he saw, he said in a sermon 'On Healing' 'was a sick people, sick as a whole and sick as individuals. Their faces are shaped by burdens too heavy to be carried, by sorrows too deep to be forgotten. And what their faces expressed, their words confirmed: tales of horror, stories of pain and despair, anxieties dwelling in their blood, confusions and self-contradictions disturbing their minds'. And, he added, there was also guilt, although this was very often hidden: 'For it hides itself under passionate denials of guilt, under self-excuse and accusations of others, under a mixture of hostility and humility, of self-pity and self-hate' (NB, 34).

That, on a large canvas, fairly represents what Tillich saw as the defining situation of those who, having separated themselves from others

DOI: 10.1057/9781137454478.0008

through the pursuit of their own absolute autonomy, find themselves seemingly trapped and unable to return to relationship. And it is a situation that, again following classical Lutheranism, he sees diagnosed in the apostle Paul's experience of being unable to do the good that he wants to do and doing instead the evil that he does not want to do, as if what Paul calls 'sin' has taken over his capacity for moral agency.[12] This situation is one of despair, which Tillich describes as 'the agony of being responsible for the loss of the meaning of one's existence and being unable to recover it' (ST2, 87).

In this situation, then, a significant part of the pain is to do with this last element, that is, that we are or feel ourselves unable to make our own way back into relationship so as to reconnect with others, with our world, and with ourselves. This, however, hasn't stopped human beings from developing a whole range of attempts at self-salvation, of which religion itself is a prominent instance. For, in religion, especially in the kind of religion that the gospels (fairly or not) associate with the Pharisees, human beings use such strategies as obedience to religious and moral laws, ascetic discipline, and supposed mystical experiences as means of persuading themselves that they have come back into a right relation to God. Now Tillich doesn't necessarily disparage any of these strategies, but the point is that none of them can work in and of themselves and they cannot work if they become separated out from the flow of life, of freedom and destiny, and become – paradoxically enough – autonomous systems that function to produce good believers or loyal followers of one or other Church.

This is why the power that is active in salvation is and must be a power 'not ourselves' yet, as in Tillich's account of the relationship between spirit and Spirit, it must be a power that can be 'in' us even as it carries us ecstatically beyond ourselves. The fundamental point here is that 'Man, in relation to God, cannot do anything without him. He must receive in order to act. New being precedes new acting' (ST2, 92).

The dialectical conditions of this situation are by now becoming familiar. 'New being' is not of course 'novelty being'. It is not 'new' in the sense of being without precedent or relation to what has gone before. But it is new in the sense that it re-news our grounding in the power of being-itself at the point at which that had seemingly vanished – in this case, obscured by the depths of self-loathing of the person gripped by despair. It is theonomous power working, no matter how hidden, in the strife and struggle of the would-be autonomous self.

DOI: 10.1057/9781137454478.0008

The proximity of theonomy and autonomy in this situation can be shown in the reformulation of the traditional doctrine of justification as a matter of acceptance. Faced with the autonomous individual striving for self-assertion, Tillich argues that the religious response should not be to call for the subjection or even the annihilation of the would-be autonomous self, but, precisely, to enable self-acceptance on the part of the self that believes it has become unacceptable. If this has the character of 'in spite of' that Tillich repeatedly emphasizes, it is, nevertheless, acceptance and acceptance precisely of the self whose self-loathing constitutes the problem being addressed. 'He must accept acceptance', says Tillich (ST2, 206). As he puts it in the sermon 'You Are Accepted': "'You are accepted. You are accepted, accepted by that which is greater than you and the name of which you do not know. Do not ask for the name now ... Do not try to do anything now ... Do not seek for anything ... Simply accept the fact that you are accepted!'"(SF, 162).

As an example of what this means Tillich takes the story told in chapter 7 of Luke's Gospel. This tells how, when Jesus had been invited to dinner in the house of one Simon, a Pharisee, a woman known for her notorious sinfulness bursts in (Tillich, following a widespread tradition, takes her to be a prostitute). Simon and his other pharisaical guests are shocked when she falls at Jesus' feet, anoints them with oil, and wipes them clean with her hair. Jesus then turns, rebukes them, and listing what the woman has done for him, concludes 'her sins, which are many, are forgiven, for she loved much; but he who is forgiven little, loves little'.[13]

Tillich uses this story to sum up what being accepted in spite of being unacceptable means. First, he says, it must be unconditional. We cannot earn forgiveness by being righteous, or even by performing 'righteous' acts of contrition for our sins. The woman, he says, didn't come to Simon's house because she sought forgiveness, but because she knew that she would be forgiven and accepted by Jesus. His love – the power of the New Being – therefore comes first, but what it shows is that, as Tillich puts it, 'his love is the law of our own being, and that ... is the law of reuniting love' (SF, 159). The kinds of torments of conscience that Luther experienced are not, as Luther himself supposed, the workings of divine wrath but are signs of the love that, in Tillich's words, 'tries to destroy within us everything which is against love'. And, he adds, 'To love this love is to love God' (SF, 159). Finally, loving this love also means becoming able 'to accept life and to love it' (SF, 159). Knowing oneself to be

DOI: 10.1057/9781137454478.0008

accepted enables self-acceptance and self-acceptance fits us to become more accepting of others.

All of this may sound familiar because of the extent to which this approach has permeated normal secular therapeutic practice.[14] But it may also seem – as some people feel about the contemporary therapy culture in general – that it is all too focused on the inner crises of individuals and, as such, reflects just the kind of bourgeois individualism that, in his socialist period, Tillich would have seen as distracting us from the real challenges of the day.

One answer to this objection is to note that Tillich had already been actively interested in what he referred to generically as depth-psychology during the 1920s and early 1930s. Like other left-wing thinkers associated with the Frankfurt School he saw significant connections between individual neurosis and social problems. What Adorno would call 'the authoritarian personality' is a product of distorted social relationships and contributes to reinforcing them. Social transformation and personal therapy are not intrinsically alternatives and the fact that we are used to seeing them in oppositional terms is once more a reflection of how the interdependent structures of individualization and participation become distorted and turned into structures of destruction under the conditions of existence (in this case, the conditions of bourgeois society). The healing of individuals empowers them to become free from the false consciousness of the prevailing social order and therefore free also to struggle against it whilst the struggle for social transformation is aimed at a future state of affairs in which individuals are no longer prevented from flourishing by poverty, injustice, environmental degradation and other social ills. We learn to love so as to bring about a social order of love. Love is both means and end. It is perhaps interesting in this connection, then, that when Tillich preaches on 'The Power of Love' he no longer talks in abstract concepts about the ontological constitution of the individual but simply tells the story of a human life in which the power of love was made manifest. His example is Elsa Brandström, the daughter of a Swedish Ambassador to Russia who gave up her privileged life to care for German prisoners of war in Siberia during the First World War and, after the war, worked for the orphans of both German and Russian prisoners until, like Tillich himself, she was forced to leave Germany by the National Socialist seizure of power. For Tillich, this was, simply, what it meant to live a life that made God 'transparent in every moment' (NB, 28). 'For God is love,' he concludes,

DOI: 10.1057/9781137454478.0008

'And in every moment of genuine love we are dwelling in God and God in us' (NB, 29).

Does Tillich's teaching on love lead us beyond the limits of a system of identity and beyond onto-theology? Or is he still thinking the kind of love manifest in a woman such as Elsa Brandström in terms of a dialectic of unity-disunity-reconciliation that has become virtually formulaic? Being or love? *Esse* or *agape*?

As I argued at the beginning of this chapter, this is not only a question that bedevils the interpretation of Tillich; it is also a question that cuts deep into the Christian tradition itself. But to stay with Tillich there is one more factor that we need to take into account before offering a tentative answer to these questions and that is what we might call the question of communication, a question that encompasses both Tillich's own explicit theories, the relationship between language, symbolism, and being, his method of correlation, and his own practice as a Christian communicator. It is to these issues that the next and final chapter will be devoted.

Notes

1 Heidegger, *Being and Time*, p. 19.
2 Tillich is himself aware that the issue is more fundamental than whether or not the word 'love' is used to describe the ultimate unity of all things in the system. In Spinoza and Hegel, for example, he saw examples of systematic thinkers who certainly used the word 'love' to express the coinherence of all things but for whom the driving force of their thought was nevertheless systematic unity rather than the kind of personal act with which the word love is usually associated.
3 Feuerbach is a notable example, but, with some qualification, the same could be said of, for example, Kant.
4 It might be objected that although this might apply in the case of romantic love, it doesn't apply to the kind of love that is manifested in works of charity. Here too, however, experience seems to suggest that where such charity is exercised solely on a generic basis it can easily be felt by the recipient as 'cold' charity. In situations of extreme emergency it may be overridingly important just to get material supplies to those who need them, but as soon as the acute crisis is over then other needs come to the fore and these include the need of those being helped to have the uniqueness of their voice and situation listened to.

DOI: 10.1057/9781137454478.0008

5   A striking example of this is the relationship between the Bishop and Emilie in Ingmar Bergman's film *Fanny and Alexander*. Emilie is attracted to the Bishop because he represents the constancy she craves, having, as she herself says, lost her sense of who she is amongst all the manifold roles she has played in her career as an actress. He, however, as he too realizes, is playing a role, but he has just one role and has become so identified with it that he cannot give it up without ceasing to be himself. Inevitably, the relationship ends badly: each exemplifies a possible form of disintegration and their coming together reinforces rather than reconciles their separate disintegration.

6   In then contemporary usage, the structure of what we would call moral laws prevalent in a society at any given point would be its 'ethical life' (*Sittlichkeit*), although usage is more flexible in German (as in English) than philosophers sometimes would like to admit.

7   *Agape* is the Greek New Testament word for love, as in such expressions as 'God is love' or 'Love is the fulfilling of the Law'.

8   From the Greek *auto-nomos*, being one's own law.

9   From the Greek *hetero-nomos*, the law of another.

10   Berdyaev commented that the lack of a strongly developed sense of moral autonomy is a defining feature of Russian culture, a point that continues to be debated today in relation to the fragility of human rights legislation in post-Soviet as well as in Soviet Russia.

11   In P. Tillich, ed. M. J. Thomas, *The Spiritual Situation in Our Technical Society* (Macon, GA: Mercer University Press, 1988), p. 183. See also the reference to my *Thinking about God in an Age of Technology* in Note 12 in Chapter 3.

12   See, for example, the sermon 'The Good that I will, I do not' based on the key text of Paul's *Letter to the Romans*, chapter 7, verses 19–20 in EN, 40–9.

13   This story is also central to Kierkegaard's account of forgiveness as the healing of despair. For discussion see my *Kierkegaard and the Theology of the Nineteenth Century* (Cambridge: Cambridge University Press, 2013), pp. 150–61. Cf. Tillich's comment that Kierkegaard's *The Sickness unto Death* offers 'the most impressive description of the situation of despair' (STII, 87), although Kierkegaard's interpretation of the story of the sinful woman in fact puts more emphasis than Tillich does on *her* initiative and her love as eliciting ('loving forth', as he puts it), Jesus' love to her.

14   Rollo May and Carl Rogers are just two of the significant figures in this movement who were influenced by Tillich. R. D. Laing owned the first two volumes of the *Systematic Theology* and *The Courage to Be*.

DOI: 10.1057/9781137454478.0008

5
The Shaking of the Foundations

Abstract: *Tillich's sermons can be approached as a non-technical exposition of what we find in his systematic theology. Sermonic discourse as understood by Tillich is, however, of a different kind from that which we engage in when we attempt to think systematically. Tillichian preaching is neither dogmatic assertion nor moral exhortation but sets out existential possibilities in the optative mode and, as Tillich understands it, the preacher has to be someone who shares the uncertainties and anxieties of the congregation. This can be seen as exemplifying his notion of theology as answering to the questions of its audience or as correlated to the significant symbols and images of contemporary culture. Preaching aims to make love possible.*

Pattison, George. *Paul Tillich's Philosophical Theology: A Fifty-Year Reappraisal.* Basingstoke: Palgrave Macmillan, 2015. DOI: 10.1057/9781137454478.0009.

Although the highly abstract and Germanic philosophical style of the *Systematic Theology* and Tillich's other academic works were often off-putting to many Anglo-Saxon readers, some of Tillich's work did find a wide readership, especially *The Courage to Be* (continuously in print since its first publication in 1952) and the three volumes of sermons: *The Shaking of the Foundations, The Eternal Now,* and *The New Being.* Tillich himself is said to have encouraged those who had difficulty in understanding his *Systematic Theology* to turn, instead to his sermons: 'First read my sermons!'[1]

But there are several ways of taking this advice. One might be to assume that the sermons are simply popular adaptations of what is said in the *Systematic Theology* and that whilst the latter is aimed at an audience of academic specialists the sermons set out the same ideas in popular or semi-popular language. On this basis, readers might go to the sermons in order to get an introduction to the systematic theology underpinning them. This is not entirely misguided. Those who have read the *Systematic Theology* will recognize many of the themes and expressions found in the sermons – and in the course of this book too, I have from time to time turned to the sermons to gloss one or other topic from the more academic part of Tillich's work. However, there is more to it than that. Precisely because preaching is a completely different genre from academic writing it has the potential to say things that cannot be said in academic work. Of course, there are many examples of preachers who fail to recognize this and whose sermons are really just lectures of a more or less popular kind. But because it is a word spoken face-to-face, or 'live' speech, by a living subject to other living subjects and because it not only concerns the truth of a set of propositions but also challenges both speaker and listeners with regard to the defining existential decisions of their lives, the sermon can and arguably should move into very different territory from the objectivity and neutrality of most academic work.[2]

This difference can, of course, be used to justify the heteronomous modes of authoritarian preaching, when the preacher takes it upon himself to instruct the passive congregation in what they should or shouldn't believe or do, whether on the basis of scriptural authority or ecclesiastical tradition. From Tillich's point of view, however, this would be precisely the sort of move we might expect from history's Grand Inquisitors. Alternatively, we might interpret this difference as justifying a preacher in abandoning all canons of evidence-based reasoning

DOI: 10.1057/9781137454478.0009

as he attempts to inspire the congregation with apocalyptic or mystical insights into obscure heavenly truths. Again, however – and despite his acknowledgement of the ecstatic character of existence – this would not be a route we can imagine Tillich wanting to go down, not least because such preaching would divert from the concrete existential situation in which the word is being spoken and to which it is being addressed.

Both these ways of using preaching's potential for authoritarian or irrational abuses are remote from what makes it a vital interpretative key in relation to Tillich. Where they seem to put the preacher above criticism, the Tillichian sermon places the preacher alongside his listeners as one who shares their existential anxieties, failures in courage, and doubts. In the second of three sermons on 'The Theologian' Tillich comments as follows on the apostle Paul's statement that 'to the weak became I as weak': 'We can become weak by having the strength to acknowledge our weakness, by restraining ourselves from all fanaticism and theological self-certainty, and by participating – not from the outside, but from the inside – in the weakness of all those to whom we speak as theologians'. And, he adds, 'Nothing is more disastrous for the theologian himself and more despicable to those whom he wants to convince than a theology of self-certainty' (SF, 125). Preaching itself will therefore be a form of discourse in which self-questioning, uncertainty, and risk – not to mention potential controversy and dispute – are integral to what is being said and to how it must be said.

These last comments not only build in a certain protection against preaching's heteronomous tendencies, but they also point to why the sermons have an important role in relation to our overall interpretation of Tillich's theology. At several points in this study, I have raised the question as to whether, in the end, Tillich's theology really goes beyond the logic of identity that we discerned in Schelling's metaphysical system. Even if Tillich, following the later Schelling, reworks this as a pattern of identity – separation – reconciliation, it all too often seems that the dice are always loaded in favour of the return to identity. The system seems to function like an elastic band that, no matter how far we stretch it (and, in Tillich's case, this is very far), always snaps back into place. In our so-called postmodern age, an age which stresses difference and alterity, this must seem a weakness. However, the comments we have just read in the sermon on 'The Theologian' invite another reading and it is this other reading that we shall pursue further in this chapter. This will not only help us see how the system is very different from any kind of theological

DOI: 10.1057/9781137454478.0009

calculating machine or dogmatic textbook, in which all the answers are listed before the first question ever gets asked. It will also help us see how the element of identity itself, the aspect of 'already' in the formula 'already – not yet' can offer a powerful homiletic and pastoral resource.

Before coming to the sermons themselves, however, we shall look at several relevant aspects of Tillich's understanding of language and communication, specifically his theory of symbols and his idea of the question-and-answer structure of Christian communication, a structure that is integral to his method of correlation. By doing so, we shall see that the effect of the sermons is very much in accord with his own theoretical reflections on how the spiritual power of the New Being might be communicated and made present to those afflicted by the structures of destruction.

Spirit, sacrament, symbol

One of the traditional fault lines between Protestant and Catholic theologies has been that, following Luther, Protestantism rejected whatever support philosophy might offer to faith in favour of 'Scripture alone', to quote the Reformers' own slogan: *sola Scriptura*. Although Catholicism has consistently maintained its long-standing view that philosophy offers an appropriate prolegomenon to 'sacred science', Karl Barth's especially powerful formulation of the distinction between faith and reason led to the rejection of philosophy becoming a dominating feature of Protestant theology in the mid-twentieth century. Tillich, as we have seen, constitutes a significant exception to this general picture on account of the way in which he incorporates German Idealism into his basic theological vision. A further confessional fault-line between Protestantism and Catholicism is the Protestant emphasis on 'the Word', that is, the word of scripture and preaching, and the Catholic emphasis on sacrament,[3] and here too Tillich goes a long way towards what might be regarded as a 'Catholic' approach, particularly apparent in the privileged place he gives to visual art. For although it has rarely been claimed that visual art as such is sacramental, the sacramental principle that created matter is capable of bearing divine meaning has been broadly assumed to be welcoming to the range of artistic expressions that expand and mediate the scriptural and sacramental expressions of ecclesiastical faith. On this basis a welcoming attitude towards the arts is widely seen as a 'Catholic'

DOI: 10.1057/9781137454478.0009

trait, with Protestant iconoclasm representing the opposite tendency. Again, Tillich seems in this regard to be closer to a more 'Catholic' position. Nevertheless, his attitude to art and to the sacraments is by no means conventionally Catholic and, in the end, he too insists on the primacy of the word.

Tillich's discussion of word and sacrament comes in a section of the *Systematic Theology* entitled 'The Spiritual Presence'. As we saw in Chapter 4, Tillich resisted the Barthian attempt to undo the nineteenth century's emphasis on the human spirit as indicating a certain divine potential in humanity. Acknowledging that the term spirit had become 'almost forbidden' (ST3, 118) in theological circles, Tillich nevertheless affirmed that despite the demonic horrors unleashed by human sin, the best element in human life did retain a kinship with the divine and that the human spirit, with a small 's', could be expressive of divine Spirit, Holy Spirit – although, as he also insisted, this would require the human spirit to be ecstatically transformed and led beyond itself by the irruption of divine Spirit. But in what ways, then, might human spirit become expressive of divine Spirit and in what human media might the divine Spirit manifest itself as present?

These questions lead Tillich to the topic of word and sacrament which he accepts as indicating the two basic forms such manifestation might take, commenting that this represents 'the primordial phenomenon that reality is communicated either by the silent presence of the object as object or by the vocal self-expression of a subject to a subject' (ST3, 128). Commenting on this, he immediately adds that, of the two, 'the sacrament is "older" than the Word' (ST3, 128). It is 'older' in the sense that sacramental expression is essentially material and relates to instinctive and unconscious dimensions of life, dimensions that in the individual and in the species pre-exist the emergence of linguistically mediated and fully and reflexively self-conscious life. Or, to put it more simply, it is 'older' in the sense that it is *pre*-verbal. We do not need words to feel the significance of washing with water or eating bread and drinking wine, to take the examples of baptism and communion. So too, painting, dance, and sculpture communicate something important, even if they are wordless.

These last examples are important because it is one of Tillich's services to modern theology to have broadened the discussion of sacramental life beyond the traditional and often acrimonious debates between Catholic and Protestant theologians as to the number of sacraments and their

DOI: 10.1057/9781137454478.0009

precise theological justification and ecclesiastical administration and use. As Tillich says, 'The largest sense of the term [sacramental] denotes everything in which the Spiritual presence has been experienced' (ST3, 128–9).[4] Any aspect of our material worldly life can become sacramental, although not everything will, nor will everything be equally sacramental for everyone or even for the same person at different periods of life. A piece of music or a landscape that I once experienced as deeply spiritually significant may lose its power to express spiritual presence and, conversely, something I once regarded as being of no real significance may become 'sacramental' (as a child, I found rows of ancient pottery in museums boring: now I find them more spiritually expressive than most works of Renaissance art; others will have comparable though perhaps opposite experiences).

Tillich, then, was deeply aware of and committed to emphasizing the importance and power of pre-verbal means of communication. Nevertheless, he also goes on to add that if sacramental objects are somehow 'older' than the word 'the word is the Spirit's other and ultimately more important medium' (ST3, 132). Why? Because although the material dimension of life finds spiritual expression in sacramental forms, it cannot of itself fully articulate what is proper and distinctive to human being, namely, our subjective self-consciousness, our sense of freedom and responsibility, and, implicit in that, our transcendence of merely material existence. Something 'more' is needed, and that something 'more' is what is given in language.

As in the case of sacraments, however, Tillich wants to expand the sense of 'word' beyond its conventional theological associations of scripture and preaching. The word is only a medium of spiritual presence when it really does mediate spiritual presence, and it is not only the words of scripture and theology that do that. Nevertheless, he also comments that the biblical word does offer a criterion by which the spiritual communicativeness of all human words can be judged, namely, that 'Nothing is the Word of God if it contradicts the faith and love which are the work of the Spirit and which constitute the New Being as it is manifest in Jesus as the Christ' (ST3, 133). Just as a painting of a scene from the life of Jesus may lack the expressive power to make it genuinely expressive of the power of the New Being, even the words of scripture cannot be guaranteed to have this power and in certain contexts and on certain occasions it may be that other, non-scriptural terms will do a better job. It is not a question of literal content but of symbolic power.

DOI: 10.1057/9781137454478.0009

The idea of the 'symbol' is a major feature of Tillich's discussion of religious and Christian communication. In his terms, word and sacrament are both symbolic forms of communication. Religious truth cannot be known directly and objectively in the manner of scientific truth since religious truth is inseparable from the human subject's own quest for meaning and salvation. As we have several times heard Tillich say, that God is Being-Itself is the one non-symbolic statement we can make about God, that is, the one statement that is literally and directly true. Beyond this, everything else is symbolic – including, it seems, all the favoured terms in which Christianity is accustomed to articulate its idea of God: Father, Trinity, person, creator, judge, and so on. That all such expressions are symbolic means, Tillich says, that they are indirect and point to something beyond themselves. At the simplest level this is because they try to express ultimate reality in terms of images, experiences, ideas, or events drawn from finite human experience. But finite human experience cannot adequately express the fullness of infinite divine Being. At the same time, because everything is as it is because of its participation in Being-Itself and in the structures by which Being-Itself sustains and shapes all that exists, it is never without some relation to Being-Itself. This means that, despite being drawn from finite life and experience, a symbol can express something of that which grounds it and to which it is always in some kind of relation, no matter how fractured or distorted.

Crucial for Tillich is the fact that, as opposed to signs, symbols are not purely conventional. In much the same way that we are gripped by the power of a work of art without being able to explain why, so too a symbol addresses and affects us in a way that cannot be calculated in advance or ever fully rationalized. In now familiar terms, a symbol expresses a theonomous state of mind – but precisely for that reason it will always evade the attempts of the autonomous self to explain or manage it. Indeed, Tillich says, symbols have a life and death that is beyond rational control. It is not only individuals but also cultures that are differently affected by the same symbols at different stages of their development. Amongst the symbols that Tillich discusses in this regard are fatherhood and kingship and, as he suggests, these are only effective symbols for God if our normal, finite experience of fatherhood or kingship has a 'holy' character. But, precisely with regard to these key elements in the Christian vocabulary, it is clear that this is culturally variable. A symbol that at one point in history, or in one culture, seems spontaneously and unproblematically to speak of God may lose its power and be perhaps

DOI: 10.1057/9781137454478.0009

replaced by other symbols that relate more directly to our own human experience of what is holy. Motherhood supplements and perhaps even replaces fatherhood, and the idea of a 'democracy to come' (Derrida) replaces the idea of kingship.[5] The old symbols may live on in liturgy and popular piety, but they have lost all or some of their original power. *The Courage to Be* seems to suggest that even the word 'God' may have lost its power for those who have lived through the intellectual, social, and cultural crises of modernity and that whatever 'God' remains as the object of any existentially possible religious faith will be a God 'beyond the God of theism'. If not technically dead, the term 'God' has been drained of much of the power it once expressed. Where eighteenth-century printing conventions might require the adjuration of God to be replaced by a hyphen or asterisk, no expression is more globally ubiquitous today than OMG. Perhaps there can be few clearer examples of the life and death of symbols.

The term 'power' is itself crucial in Tillich's understanding of symbol. For the point of a religious symbol is not that it adequately defines or describes God. It doesn't and cannot, since (apart from the intrinsic impossibility of defining or describing God) definition and description are not the aim of religious communication. This aim is rather to confirm or to induct human beings into an existential relation to God, that is, to experience the power of the new being and to help that power become effective in their lives.[6] This, importantly, can be seen as related to Tillich's ideas of the demonic. As we saw in the case of his call to the German people to make 'the socialist decision', the demonism of a power such as Nazism can never be defeated by reason alone but only be a power that is greater than itself. It is this power that we may variously gloss as the power of love or the courage to be that Christian teaching in general and preaching in particular seek to communicate.

Preaching the word

There are many points at which what Tillich says about sacrament, word, and symbol can, and perhaps needs to, be challenged with regard to its theological and philosophical import. Here, however, what has been said has been directed at introducing some closing reflections on Tillich's practice as a preacher. However, as we shall see, these reflections also help us see aspects of his philosophical theology in a new light.

DOI: 10.1057/9781137454478.0009

What should be immediately clear is that Tillich never construed the task of preaching as essentially a matter of *teaching*. In other words, preaching is not a popular version of a theological lecture and the main point is not to communicate an idea, clarify a problem of doctrine, or resolve an apparent contradiction in the text. The main point is, precisely, a matter of courage: to communicate the courage to be, to love, and to hope. This may involve explaining ideas, clarifying problems, or dealing with textual issues along the way, but these are incidental to the central aim.

Another way of putting this is to say that the language of preaching is not indicative but imperative. Preaching is not about telling those who are listening what is the case but confronting them with ethical or existential possibilities. We have already noted the risk of preaching being construed or at least perceived as liable to heteronomous abuse and, certainly, popular cultural representations of preaching seem to assume that preaching normally involves the self-understanding of the preacher as someone 12 feet above criticism. In the situation of theonomy however – that is, when the message really does convey the power of New Being – the power of preaching has nothing to do with the authority of the preacher but with the power of a spiritual presence to which the preacher as well as the congregation is essentially subordinate. This doesn't entirely remove the risk of heteronomous abuse, however, since we can easily imagine (perhaps we have even experienced) preachers using the claim that it's not their own words but God's Word that matters as a means of reinforcing their authority over the congregation – whether deliberately or by dint of a simple lack of awareness of the psychological dynamics of the situation.

Of course, as we have heard with regard to Tillich's appeal to Paul's saying that 'To the weak became I as weak', the theologian must participate 'not from the outside, but from the inside' in the weakness, that is, the intellectual and existential uncertainty of those to whom he speaks. 'We are strong,' he adds, 'only in so far as we point, for our own sake, and for the sake of others, to the truth which possesses us, but which we do not possess' (SF, 125). In these terms, each sermon is itself a struggle for the faith to which it calls its listeners.

If this is taken as a guideline for understanding Tillich's own practice as a preacher, then it throws new light on his much discussed method of correlation. From the 1920s onwards Tillich had sought to develop what he called an 'answering' theology; that is, a theology that answered

DOI: 10.1057/9781137454478.0009

the needs of the actual present situation. He later formalized this principle into a 'method of correlation' by which theological answers were correlated with existential questions and theological concepts with philosophical concepts. An obvious example is how, in his religious socialism, Tillich correlated the theological promise of the Kingdom of God with the Marxist struggle for a classless society. Another would be how the anxiety revealed in expressionist art pointed to the quest for a new power of Being. Thus, as Tillich himself puts it, 'The Christian message provides the answers to the questions implied in human existence' (ST1, 72). However, this way of putting it, reinforced by his subsequent statement that the theological answer cannot be inferred from the existential question (ST2, 14), might seem to return us to the situation of the heteronomous preacher who has all the answers that his congregation are unable to give themselves. But this would then seem to cancel Tillich's own claim that the theologian participates from the inside in the questions and uncertainties to which he responds and is not merely an 'outside' commentator on them. And, in fact, the *Systematic Theology* itself goes on from affirming the independence of the theological answer to speak also of a certain *inter*dependence of question and answer. This, however, suggests that the theologian is not someone who 'has' the answer but one who is always struggling for it (ST2, 16–17) and it also means that, as Tillich says, 'the form of the theological answer is not independent of the form of the existential question' and that we 'receive and express [the answer] according to the way [we] asked for it' (ST2, 17).

And there is one further point we must take into account. As we have now many times seen, the principle of identity underlying Tillich's system means that no matter how extreme the disruption of the structures of Being, nothing that in any way exists is ever entirely cut off from the power of Being-Itself. It may be estranged, subject to demonic perversion, and brought to the brink of annihilation, but it is not and never can be 'nothing'. But this means, as Tillich himself puts it, that even despair about the meaninglessness of life presupposes that it is meaningful to raise the question of meaning. The one who raises the question will therefore always have some anticipatory sense of what the answer might or could be, what the Catholic theologian Karl Rahner called a *Vorgriff* or pre-hension of the God concealed in the mystery of Being.[7]

In bringing the existential demand and the existential encouragement of the word of preaching to the congregation, therefore, the preacher stands before the people as equally finite, equally fallible, and equally subject to anxiety. Rather than simply seeing the language of preaching as 'imperative', then, we might do better to think of it as optative, that is, a grammatical mode that finds expression in such sayings as 'May it be so!' or 'Let's go and play!' Such optative imperatives do not tell listeners what they *must* do but what they may, might, or could do and therefore they suppose, invite, and require the freedom of the listener to be activated in agreeing to, or acting upon, what has been said. Preacher and listener are co-involved in developing and pre-hending the possibility that is to be presented as an 'answer' and it is because of this prehension that she/he is able to apprehend it as meaningful to and transformative of his or her own life. Philosophically, the optative mode answers the ontological category of possibility or potentiality (and, perhaps, to what Schelling called 'potency') – which, in a certain perspective, is another way of saying 'power'. As a kind of performative utterance, the sermon – comprising both delivery and reception – performs the moment of unrealized potentiality (i.e. the moment of openness and undecideness) inherent that is inseparable from every affirmation of being and in every call to action, the 'not yet' in the 'now'.

Tillich himself does not, as far as I know, develop any theory of the grammar of preaching, but I suggest that this idea of preaching as speaking in the empowering mode of the optative imperative throws significant light on his actual practice. Sometimes, indeed, he ends a sermon with just such an explicitly optative summons. The sermon from which the collection *The Shaking of the Foundations* takes its name ends like this: 'In these days the foundations of the earth *do* shake. May we not turn our eyes away; may we *not* close our ears and our mouths! But may we rather see, through the crumbling of a world, the rock of eternity and the salvation which has no end!' (SF, 11) However, we should not be over-literal about this. There are other sermons that, in terms of their surface grammar, seem to end in straightforwardly indicative assertions, such as the sermon 'The Two Servants of Yahweh', which ends: 'We can find the solution to the riddle of history as a whole, and of our particular history, in the figure of Cyrus in the service of the servant of Yahweh' (SF, 33).[8] In the context of sermonic discourse, however, such statements are better read or understood as if they are speaking in something like the optative mode. In this case, the meaning would be in the direction of 'May we therefore trust that, however improbably, historical convulsions may still become the occasion for good.' In

DOI: 10.1057/9781137454478.0009

the context of sermonic speech, the formally indicative statement has optative force – precisely because the preacher shares the existential situation of the listeners and speaks not as an agent of heteronomous power but as a witness to possibilities of faith, hope, and love that are not immediately evident in either the preacher's or the listener's life experience.

These comments put us in a position to address a question that has been simmering since Chapter 1. There I drew attention to how Tillich's Schellingian insistence on the persistence of identity in relation to difference seemed to distance him from the characteristic post-Heideggerian and post-modern emphasis on difference. In the context of the sermon, however, this assertion of identity takes on a different character. In the domain of systematic theology or philosophy, the principle of identity asserts a principle of Being, that is, an assertion of what is the case, always, everywhere, and invariably – and that is what is asserted also in Tillich's system. If, however, we regard the system not as the apex of Tillich's life-work but as subordinate to the practice of preaching, a rather different view emerges. For in the context of preaching, the assertion of identity is no longer the assertion of what is the case, but it is a call involving witness, challenge, and courageous response. It is no longer a given, but a matter of possibility. And in this context too, we can see that it 'says' what, perhaps, Christian preaching must always 'say' if it is to call forth the courage that it commends.

A number of Tillich's sermons seem especially to emphasize that, in a certain sense, we are 'always already' in relation to the power of being that we seek or that our transient, historical existence is, despite appearances, grounded in a relation to the Eternal. So, in the sermon 'We Live in Two Orders', Tillich says that the two orders of history and the eternal 'are within each other'. Therefore, he concludes, 'We are not a lost generation because we are a suffering, destroyed generation. Each of us belongs to the eternal order, and the prophet speaks to all of us: Comfort ye, comfort ye, my people' (SF, 23). In 'The Depth of Existence', similarly, he speaks of the eternal joy that is always present in the depths, even when the surface of our lives seems far from eternity and far from joy (SF, 63). Perhaps an especially striking example is the sermon 'The Meaning of Providence' on the text of Romans 8.38–39, 'For I am persuaded, that neither death, nor life, nor angels, nor principalities, nor powers, nor things present, nor things to come, nor height, nor depth, nor any other creature, shall be able to separate

DOI: 10.1057/9781137454478.0009

us from the love of God, which is in Christ Jesus our Lord.' Here Tillich argues that

> the content of the faith in Providence is this: when death rains from heaven as it does now, when cruelty wields power over nations and individuals as it does now, when hunger and persecution drive millions from place to place as they do now, and when prisons and slums all over the world distort the humanity of the bodies and souls of men as they do now – we can boast in that time, and just in that time, that even all of this cannot separate us from the love of God. In this sense, and in this sense alone, all things work together for good, for the *ultimate* good, the eternal love, and the Kingdom of God. Faith in divine Providence is the faith that nothing can prevent us from fulfilling the ultimate meaning of our existence. Providence does not mean a divine planning by which everything is predetermined, as is an efficient machine. Rather, Providence means that there is a creative and saving possibility implied in every situation, which cannot be destroyed by any event. Providence means that the daemonic and destructive forces within ourselves and our world can never have an unbreakable grasp upon us, and that the bond which connects us with the fulfilling love can never be disrupted. (SF 106–7)

Read as a statement of systematic theology, this means that the future is already within the power of the being that even now *is* and that the experience of time and of temporal alterity or difference is ultimately subordinated to the principle of Being-Itself. If, however, we read these words as sermonic speech, then we understand that they constitute an act of witness to the existential possibility that we, the listeners or readers, are called to find the power and the freedom to respond with love and hope to any situation in which we may find ourselves, no matter how extreme, humiliating, or shameful. And this is no longer to speak the language of a philosophy of identity or of ontotheology. This is the language of 'not yet' in which the moment of indeterminacy is glossed in terms of fundamental or radical hope. Perhaps, therefore, we should not read Tillich's sermons 'first', as he advised us to do, but to read them 'last', because it is in the sermons that this most systematic of systematic theologians break out of the system and let us see that everything that is said in the system is staked anew in every word that the preacher speaks to us. The 'difference' that cannot be stated in terms of the system is enacted in the uncertainty, the waiting, and the struggle to find and to enact the possibility of love that is the advent of the New Being and, in religious language, the hope of salvation.

DOI: 10.1057/9781137454478.0009

Notes

1   See the article by Erdmann Sturm, 'First, read my sermons! Tillich as Preacher' in Russell Re Manning (ed.), *The Cambridge Companion to Tillich* (Cambridge: Cambridge University Press, 2009), pp. 105–20. Purely anecdotally, I may add that I have often used extracts from classic sermons for meditation in public worship, usually after the anthem at Choral Evensong; not every text works equally well, but those that consistently got positive remarks from members of the congregation and requests for references were the sermons of John Henry Newman and Paul Tillich. Of course, their theological views could scarcely be more different, but what their preaching shares is a sense for the pace and level of preaching to a thoughtful but not necessarily academic community.

2   These comments should not be taken as implying that academic work is devoid or should be devoid of passion and commitment, merely that the mix is somewhat different in these two cases. It should also be pointed out that the majority of Tillich's English-language sermons were given in college-based contexts and therefore to congregations whose members would probably have been capable of reading the *Systematic Theology* if they had wished. This, however, illustrates from another angle that by saying it differently the sermon also says something different from what is said in the more purely academic work.

3   A classic definition of sacrament is 'an outward and visible sign of an inward and spiritual grace'. All Christian churches affirm two basic sacraments: baptism and holy communion. Roman Catholicism, however, also acknowledges the sacraments of confirmation, penance, extreme unction, ordination, and marriage. Protestantism, however, rejects these as having a sacramental character on the grounds that they are not supported by a dominical word, that is, a commandment spoken by Christ himself.

4   A more recent attempt to open up the range of what might properly be regarded as sacramental has been David Brown's three volumes *God and Enchantment of Place: Reclaiming Human Experience* (Oxford: Oxford University Press, 2004), *God and Grace of Body: Sacrament in Ordinary* (Oxford: Oxford University Press, 2007), and *God and Mystery in Words: Experience through Metaphor and Drama* (Oxford: Oxford University Press, 2008). However, it should be said that Brown is not directly influenced by Tillich in this respect, although they reach comparable positions.

5   In this regard it is striking that Mary Daly's *Beyond God the Father* attacks what she sees as Tillich's own androcentric assumptions about God. See references in Mary Daly, *Beyond God the Father: Towards a Philosophy of Women's Liberation* (Boston: Beacon Press, 1973).

6   In this regard, the complaint that Tillich's theory of the symbol does not do enough to ground cognitive claims about the nature of God is misplaced since

DOI: 10.1057/9781137454478.0009

it is not attempting to do the same kind of work as, for example, Thomas's theory of analogy.

7 'Prehension' (a term introduced into philosophy by A. N. Whitehead) is the nearest literal translation into English of Rahner's *Vorgriff* and may be rendered more idiomatically as a preliminary or anticipatory grasp of the matter at issue.

8 The reference is to Cyrus King of Persia. After his victory over Babylon in 540BCE, Cyrus allowed the Israelite people who had been forcibly exiled to Babylon to return to Palestine, thus 'serving' the servant of Yahweh, the God of Israel, by fulfilling his prophecy (deemed improbable at the time) that the exiles would indeed return to their own land.

DOI: 10.1057/9781137454478.0009

Bibliography

Anthologies of work by Tillich

Ed. J. and J. Dillenberger, *On Art and Architecture* (New York: Crossroad, 1987).
Ed. M. J. Thomas, *The Spiritual Situation in Our Technical Society* (Macon, GA: Mercer University Press, 1988).

Collected and systematic works by Paul Tillich

▶

Gesammelte Werke (Stuttgart: Evangelisches Verlagswerk, 1959), 18 volumes.
Systematic Theology, Volume 1 (Welwyn Garden City: James Nisbet, 1953).
Systematic Theology, Volume 2 (Welwyn Garden City: James Nisbet, 1957).
Systematic Theology, Volume 3 (Welwyn Garden City: James Nisbet, 1964).

Other works by Paul Tillich

The Courage to Be (London: Collins/Fontana, 1962).
The Eternal Now (London: SCM Press, 1963).
The Interpretation of History (New York: James Scribner's Sons, 1936).
Love, Power, and Justice (London: Oxford University Press, 1954).

DOI: 10.1057/9781137454478.0010

Morality and Beyond (London: Routledge and Kegan Paul, 1964).
The New Being (London: SCM Press, 1956).
Perspectives on Nineteenth and Twentieth Century Theology (London: SCM Press, 1967).
The Protestant Era (London: James Nisbet, 1951).
The Religious Situation (New York: Meridian, 1956).
The Shaking of the Foundations (London: SCM Press, 1949).
The Socialist Decision (New York: Harper and Row, 1977).

Other works

Barth, Karl, *The Epistle to the Romans* (Oxford: Oxford University Press, 1933).
Boethius, trans. V. E. Watts, *The Consolation of Philosophy* (Harmondsworth: Penguin, 1969).
Brown, David, *God and Enchantment of Place: Reclaiming Human Experience* (Oxford: Oxford University Press, 2004)
_____ *God and Grace of Body: Sacrament in Ordinary* (Oxford: Oxford University Press, 2007).
_____ *God and Mystery in Words: Experience through Metaphor and Drama* (Oxford: Oxford University Press, 2008).
Caputo, John D., *The Insistence of God. A Theology of Perhaps* (Bloomington: Indian University Press, 2013).
Daly, Mary, *Beyond God the Father. Towards a Philosophy of Women's Liberation* (Boston: Beacon Press, 1973).
Duffy, Eamon, *The Stripping of the Altars: Traditional Religion in England, 1400–1580* (Newhaven CT: Yale University Press, 1992).
Hamilton, Kenneth, *The System and the Gospel: A Critique of Paul Tillich* (London: SCM Press, 1963).
Heidegger, Martin, *Being and Time* trans. E. Robinson and J. Macquarrie (Oxford: Blackwell, 1962).
Heidegger, Martin, *Identity and Difference*, trans. Joan Stambaugh ([Dual language edition] New York: Harper and Row, 1969).
Marcuse, Herbert, *The Aesthetic Dimension* (Basingstoke: Palgrave Macmillan, 1979).
Pattison, George, *Eternal God/Saving Time* (Oxford: Oxford University Press, 2015).

DOI: 10.1057/9781137454478.0010

_____ *Kierkegaard and the Theology of the Nineteenth Century* (Cambridge: Cambridge University Press, 2013).

_____ *Thinking about God in an Age of Technology* (Oxford: Oxford University Press, 2007).

Pauck, Wilhelm and Marion, *Paul Tillich. His Life and Thought, Volume 1: Life* (London: Collins, 1977).

Simpson, Gary M., *Critical Social Theory: Prophetic Reason, Civil Society, and Christian Imagination* (Minneapolis: Fortress Press, 2002).

Sturm, Erdmann, '"First, read my sermons!" Tillich as Preacher' in Russell Re Manning (ed.), *The Cambridge Companion to Tillich*, pp. 105–20.

Thatamanil, John, 'Tillich and the postmodern' in Russell Re Manning (ed.), *The Cambridge Companion to Paul Tillich* (Cambridge: Cambridge University Press, 2009).

Winquist, Charles E., *The Surface of the Deep* (Aurora CO: Davies, 2003).

DOI: 10.1057/9781137454478.0010

Index

DOI: 10.1057/9781137454478.0011

DOI: 10.1057/9781137454478.0011

DOI: 10.1057/9781137454478.0011